Brainsquall

Brainsquall

SOUNDINGS FROM A DEEP DEPRESSION

JIM COTTER

❖ ❖ ❖

For Anne & John
with affection

Jim
Sheffield
10. XI. 97

CAIRNS PUBLICATIONS · SHEFFIELD
in association with
ARTHUR JAMES LTD · BERKHAMSTED
1997

© Jim Cotter 1997

ISBN 0 85305 422 3

Cairns Publications
47 Firth Park Avenue, Sheffield s5 6HF

Arthur James Ltd
70 Cross Oak Road, Berkhamsted, Herts HP4 3HZ

Further copies of this book
and other Cairns Publications
can be obtained from Arthur James Ltd

A catalogue record for this book is available
from the British Library

*Typeset in Adobe Janson by
Strathmore Publishing Services, London N7*

*Printed in Great Britain by
Ipswich Book Company, Ipswich, Suffolk*

Contents

With Gratitude

You kept Cairns Publications afloat and moving
through squall and doldrums.

You held the Cairnbuilder while he chipped away
at these words to give them shape,
and you kept a lookout on the weather in the bay.

Staunch as ever, and not stopping to count the cost,
you eliminated physical distance when it really mattered.

You responded to the cry for help and kept on being there.

And I have one named dedication,
to PRIMO LEVI,
Italian chemist, prisoner and survivor of Auschwitz,
coolly impassioned writer,
whose example I have tried to follow:

"Often (one writes) to free oneself from anguish ...
I have no objection to the writer driven by conflicts:
on the contrary I hope he will be able
to free himself from them in this way,
as happened to me many years ago. I ask him, however,
to make an effort to filter his anguish,
not to fling it as it is, rough and raw,
into the face of the reader:
otherwise he risks infecting others
without getting rid of it himself."

My name is JIM

I was bearing a heavy load,
angry but not expressing it,
grief-stricken but stuck with it,
afraid but burying it,
hurt by those with power,
and by those who appeared to have none.

I broke under its weight.

I was helpless,
wordless,
stripped to nothing.

Very slowly,
very, very slowly,
I began to recover.

If you have picked up this book
and paused by this page,
and have yourself been in such a place as mine,
and if we should one day meet,
we shall recognize each other.

If someone you love has broken down,
and you also feel helpless, bewildered, confused,
the glimpses in this book of what it is like
may give you courage
to keep within range,
to be alongside without anxiety,
and not to lose hope.

Preface

TOWARDS the end of May 1994 I experienced a sudden breakdown, a 'psychotic episode', followed by six months in and out of hospital with what was diagnosed as a 'severe reactive depression'. The following year was one of restless quiet before I slowly began to make contact again with the wider world.

Putting this book together has been part therapy, part pilgrimage, part gratitude that I can write again. As I do so, with the low technology of pencil and paper, scorning (at least at this stage) anything to do with the computer, I am looking at the sea and mountains of the north western outposts of Europe, and listening to the birds of this late northern spring.

What I have written will be of no use to anyone actually in the throes of a 'breakdown': reading is the last thing that would occur to you to do. But it may help those around to be tenacious: families, partners, friends, and colleagues who are shocked by what has happened and have not a clue about what to do.

There are a number of reasons why these pages tell but part of the story. In theory a video could be retrieved from a database, but to view it would be a feat of unnecessary endurance: it would mostly be boring and in any case one-eyed. What can never be told are the stories that are the ripples from the fall of a stone, the effects on others of one person's illness.

Bad memory is another reason, both the simple fact, and the effects of treatments, and the suppression of what is still too painful fully to integrate. Insofar as my early life impinges on these events, there are connections which I have made, but others have doubtless yet to surface.

An important issue is the boundary between public and private. As I write this, I am all too aware of how easy it is, however unintentionally and without malice, to betray confidences. Even when on full alert, it is very difficult to write publicly of personal, sometimes private, matters without intruding on others, and without being indulgently exhibitionist. I hope I have discerned correctly and not trespassed on the vulnerability of others or on my own.

Lastly, I may be blind to the obvious, and I may have omitted something which some readers will immediately notice. I shan't exactly enjoy having such material pointed out, but it would doubtless be to my good.

Much of this book is written as snippets of conversations between an 'I' and a 'you'. The end of such snippets is usually marked by three dots.

Sometimes the identities are clear. But I have named only those whose writings are in the public domain. They receive due acknowledgement on the pages that follow this Preface.

The others are not named. To say why, I need to explain how the conversations came about. In June last year I wrote to a number of people who had been closely involved in my illness, though by no means all of them, asking if they would write some reflections on the contact we had had, whether that was professional or personal, whether as strangers or old friends, whether in representative roles or observing them in action. I thought such reflections might contribute to our understanding of how persons, roles, and institutions interact where 'mental illness' is concerned. I thought I would 'top and tail' these contributions with a few thoughts of my own.

A year on, with a number of letters and tapes before me, I find I am much more personally engaged than I thought I would have the energy to be. So the format has changed.

The 'you' in what follows may be friend, colleague, professional carer, focus figure of institution, 'God'.

I have put the word 'God' in inverted commas somewhat deliberately. We give so many meanings to what we experience as 'divine', and my own journey into what has been very mysterious has made me more suspicious than ever of easy definitions. This book does contain some explorations of what 'faith' might imply, and some critique of the institutional aspect of religion. But it is not, I hope, over-religious in tone nor ecclesiastical in its concerns. Indeed, I have cut out some passages that were in the first draft because they savoured of 'in-house' churchy arguments, hobby horses that are better hidden elsewhere. Those with whom I have talked about the book have confirmed my own desire that it should (at least in principle!) be accessible to the widest possible readership.

And so it is that I want to thank all those who have contributed to what follows. I have had inner conversations with those I didn't ask to contribute; some, when I did ask, felt unable to do so in a way that would identify them; others, tide and time being what they are, wanted to but in the end did not. Hence no names. But my thanks go to you all, as well as to those named in the Acknowledgements. Some who read this may recognize themselves (and some of the others), but what I have written echoes what I *heard* you say, though it may not have been *what* you said.

Those who helped me in particularly personal ways during my illness I have thanked on the dedication page, also anonymously, but no less feeling for all that.

But there are a few people who have made particular contributions to the 'surrounds' of the book itself, not least those who have read the manuscript, and especially Lavinia Byrne who read the first draft and made perceptive comments. My thanks to her, and also to John Foskett, who brings to the Foreword years of experience as Chaplain to the Maudsley Hospital in London (1976–94): he has also written *Meaning in Madness*, which was published by the

SPCK in its New Library of Pastoral Care in 1984, co-written with David Lyall; a book in the same series, published in 1988, concerned with supervision and pastoral care and entitled *Helping the Helpers*; and a chapter entitled 'Christianity and Psychiatry' in the book *Psychiatry and Religion* edited by Dinesh Bhugra and published last year by Routledge.

I am grateful to Jenny Mather for permission to use a detail from her painting *Mountain Storm* on the jacket, and to Autumn Preble of Whidbey Island in Puget Sound in the United States for the black-and-white photograph which completes the cover presentation.

JIM COTTER
Sheffield and the Isle of Skye
June and September 1997

Acknowledgements

I have made reference to the following sources and I am grateful for permission to quote from those works which are still in copyright.

ASHMORE, Win, From a personal letter

AUDEN, W. H., 'For the Time Being', *Collected Poems*, Faber & Faber, 1976

BARKER, Pat, *Regeneration*, Penguin, 1992

BAXTER, James, *Jerusalem Daybook*, Price Milburn, Wellington, 1971

BURTON, Mary, *An Unfaded Garland: Meditations on Light and Silence*, Burns & Oates, 1997, and reproduced by permission of the publisher

CROSSAN, John Dominic, *Jesus: A Revolutionary Biography*, Harper, San Francisco, 1994

DEARMER, Geoffrey, *A Pilgrim's Song*, John Murray, 1993

DYER, Geoffrey, *The Missing of the Somme*, Penguin, 1995

GOFFMAN, Erving, *Stigma*, Penguin, 1968

HEIDTMANN, Peter, *Loren Eiseley, A Modern Ishmael*, Archon, Shoe String Press, North Haven, Connecticut, 1991

HERBERT, George, 'Affliction', 'The Flower', *Collected Poems*, Penguin, 1991

LEBOYER, Frederick, *Birth without Violence*, Wildwood House, 1975

LEVI, Primo, *If This Is A Man*, Bodley Head, 1966

LEVI, Primo, 'Why Does One Write?', *Other People's Trades*, Michael Joseph, 1989

MACMURRAY, John, *The Form of the Personal*, Gifford Lectures 1954–5

MARY CLARE, Sister, *Encountering the Depths*, Darton, Longman, & Todd, 1981, and reproduced by permission of the publisher

MERTON, Thomas, *The Courage for Truth: The Letters of Thomas*

Merton to Writers, ed. Christine M. Bochen. Copyright
© 1993 by the Merton Legacy Trust. Reprinted by permission
of Farrar, Straus & Giroux, Inc., New York

NEWALL, Peter, 'On being refined', *Eremos Magazine 53*,
Magazine of the Eremos Institute, 16 Masons Drive, North
Parramatta, New South Wales 2151, Australia

NIETZSCHE, Friedrich, *The Gay Science*, Preface to the second
edition, 1887

OWEN, Wilfred, 'Anthem for Doomed Youth', 'The Send-Off',
Collected Poems, Chatto and Windus, 1971

POTTER, Dennis, From a BBC Radio 4 talk on 23 February
1977, quoted in Mayne, Michael, *A Year Lost and Found*,
Darton, Longman, & Todd, 1987

RANDALL, David, From an article in the newsletter of CARA,
London

SACKS, Oliver, *Awakenings*, Duckworth, 1973

SARTON, May, *At Seventy*, Norton, New York, 1984,
© Norton, reproduced by permission

SARTON, May, *After the Stroke*, Norton, New York, 1988,
© Norton, reproduced by permission

SARTON, May, *Endgame*, Norton, New York, 1992,
© Norton, reproduced by permission

SARGEANT, David, From a letter in *Eremos Magazine 53* (see
Newall, Peter)

STYRON, William, *Darkness Visible*, Jonathan Cape, 1990

TEILHARD DE CHARDIN, Pierre, *Hymn of the Universe*, Collins,
1961

DE VRIES, Peter, *The Blood of the Lamb*, Penguin, 1969

WARNER, Sylvia Townsend, From a letter in May Sarton,
At Seventy (q.v.)

WILLIAMS, Charles, *Descent into Hell*, Eerdman, New York, 1949

WILLIAMS, Charles, *Essential Writings in Sprituality and Theology*,
ed. Charles Hepling, Cowley Publications, Cambridge,
Boston, Massachusetts, 1993

WOOD, David, *Letter 19*, Community of the Three Hours,
6 John Street, Maryport, Cumbria, CA15 6JT

Foreword

ON reading *Brainsquall* I was continuously reminded of the otherness of madness. How it separates and divides us from ourselves and from those close to us. "I went awry, from the disturbance of the cells of my brain to a lack of connection with my closest friends." This book bears fearful witness to that separateness and reaches out to embrace and embody it in the expectation of a coming communion in which there will be "neither Jew not Greek, slave nor free, male nor female". The need in our shattering world is never greater, the task never seemingly more impossible.

In her book *Madness and Social Representation* the French social psychologist Denise Jodet traces the story of a small rural community that has fostered patients from Parisian asylums throughout this century. This provided the struggling community with some economic stability, but at the cost of an almighty vigilance towards the feared contagion of madness. Although generations of patients lived intimately with local people they were as separate a group as they would have been had they remained in hospital. The author's research painstakingly unlocks the secrets of this community, buried in its unconscious customs, and demonstrates that the fear of madness, which defies all logic and reason, still reveals the way in which societies protect themselves against the 'alien'. Chastening as this message is we are left in no doubt of the fundamental divisions which separate human beings from one another and from themselves. We do live as if our survival depends upon our 'difference' from another – another individual, group, class, colour, sex, race, or pathology.

Hans Küng once wrote of religion that it was psychiatry's last taboo, and for many religious people madness is much the same. Any discourse which attempts to draw these worlds of difference into conversation has to take seriously this reality and recognize that with human beings the task is impossible, but with God there may be just a chance. After all they called Jesus mad. There have not been many who have risked leaving the safety of these taboos in order to discover what it is they protect us from. Jim Cotter joins a small but noble band of pilgrims to stand by us in our hour of need.

William James in his *Varieties of Religious Experience* claimed that madness and mystical experience "sprang from the same mental level ... of which so little is really known. That region contains every kind of matter: seraph and snake abide there side by side." So convinced was Anton Boisen of the spiritual significance of his own breakdown that he dedicated his life to those who suffered and to those who were willing to live and learn from that suffering, and the American pastoral care and counselling movement owes its origin to his experience. More recent work in places as diverse as the Alister Hardy Centre in Oxford and the Mental Health Foundation has testified to the spiritual fruitfulness of madness and its aftermath. "Although in the short term, the psychotics' ability to function has been seriously impaired by their experiences; over a longer period they led to dramatically spiritual 'fruits' in their lives; all of the group were deeply involved in altruistic, creative, ecological or spiritual activities." Jim Cotter confirms the significance of his experience as something not just for himself but for others: it is as if his travail leads him to embody the travail of us all and that his coming conception in this book is a fragile sign of hope for us all. Harry Williams before him recognized that religion and its rituals are but military manoeuvres in preparation for the real thing ...

Jim Cotter's account of his crossing over and of his breaking of the taboos brings a fresh voice to this often forgotten remnant. He leaves us in no doubt of the terror, misery and sacrifice involved. His expedition is without map or compass, protective clothing or guiding hand. He goes to those parts of himself and of human experience that all of us pray we will never encounter. Most often they are separated off, projected, and then treated in others less fortunate than ourselves. I could not read this book without a sense of relief that although much of it sounded like me, it was not my story. I have not been committed to an asylum or been sectioned under the Mental Health Act, and so the parts of me that could gain recognition from being where Jim has been, remain in uneasy and hidden security, stigmata that have not yet burst the skin. They will have to wait in most of us for the time when we no longer see dimly but face to face.

Jim has seen much more than he or anyone else wants to see, and his urgency in writing is to bear witness to that vision before it fades – especially to treasure those precious experiences which 'held' him while he hung on his 'crosses' and stank in his 'tombs'. They kept him in mind while he was handed over to strangers, who carried him where he did not want to go. They watched and waited and nudged him like the tugs of his imagination into calmer waters just as they had held to their attachment when the gales raged. In our dividing off of the 'alien' there is much contempt for the mental health service and their contentious medical and physical treatments. Jim leads us through his own distaste for psychiatry to uncover its extraordinary humanity, its willingness to go and be where few will follow. Like others before him he finds these 'scientific reductionists' to be people whose faith survives their failure and their ignorance, and whose hope and love can bear the frustration when their efforts go unrewarded.

Reading this book was not as awesome as I expected it to be. Jim Cotter's words and images so often ascend mounts of transfiguration. Here we have sounds from the bottom of the mountain where only prayer and fasting will suffice. Here there is the ordinary, the trivial and the not especially inspiring. But don't be mistaken. It bears all the marks not of the finished smithy product but of humanity 'twisted out of shape', of the smelting and the hammer blows. This is the whole story still in its telling. The story of God who not only *is* but *is becoming* too; no longer the answer to all our questions but the question to our many answers.

In 1945 Anton Boisen wrote about his own madness, and that of St Paul, George Fox and many of those with whom he suffered and for whom he cared, as a special kind of good news. *Brainsquall* bears the same message for our times. "In so far as we attain to any true understanding of the mentally ill, so far we shall be able to see the meaning and end of human life ... And in so far as we attain to such understanding, we should be well on the way toward building the city of brotherhood and co-operation on the place where the jungle now stands and greed and ruthless competition rule."

John Foskett
Limington, Somerset
July 1997

"Seigneur, votre mer est si grande,
et ma barque est si petite."

Introduction: *Squall and Cellar*

"A TRUE wimp of a word for such a major illness." I could have hugged you, William Styron, when I read your criticism of the label 'depression'. Amusement vied with anger when you went on to compare the word to a slug "slithering innocuously through the language ... leaving little trace of its malevolence, and preventing by its very insipidity, a general awareness of the horrible intensity of the disease when out of control."

We use the word to describe a downturn in the economy or a dip in the road. We get nearer to an analogy with the weather forecast of a depression moving north-eastwards and deepening quickly, perhaps into a tropical cyclone or hurricane.

From that clue, it is a modest jump to 'brainstorm'. But such a word is compromised by its meaning of a creative technique for pooling and sifting ideas, however irrelevant they may at first seem, by a group of people faced with a problem.

As ever, I was on the hunt for a new word. 'Brain-tempest'? 'Brain-typhoon'? Or reclaiming the nineteenth century coinage 'Brain fever'? Or even, on the analogy of 'cloudburst', 'brainburst'? That was too reminiscent of bullets and gangster movies.

Then I thought of a 'squall'. There is, meteorologically, a black squall, with a rapid buildup of dark clouds giving warning. But more apt is a white squall, a sudden violent tempest whipped up seemingly from nowhere, 'out of the blue', wreaking havoc and threatening destruction to everything in its path. It may not last long: the effects of its passing last a very long time. It is the opposite of the squally showers of an English April.

My mast cracked and fell. My rudder snapped. I was 'unhelmed' (thank you again, William Styron). The good ship Jim nearly foundered. A few sturdier ships were nearby, like tugs to nudge me towards calmer waters. Storms came and went twice more before I settled, becalmed, in the doldrums. Or was I towed into harbour for a lengthy job of repair in dry dock? Either way, in time the faint whispers of wind stirred, zephyrs which spoke of some trails of meaning in the awful story, and now, as I write, the ship is riding the breezes in the bay, the wind filling its patchwork quilt of a sail, helmsman and crew keeping a careful eye on the weather and making sure they do not yet venture out of sight of land ...

So 'Brainsquall' is the title of this book, and the various stages of my life during the past three years are given these pegs on which to hang some thoughts: turbulence, squall, doldrums, zephyrs, breezes. A little fanciful, but I suppose we human beings are always seeking to bring order out of chaos, to give hints of meaning by telling and musing on our stories. Much of the time I was ill seems wasted and meaningless (more of that later), and parts of this book can at best be snapshots, taken in the dark water with an inefficient camera. Photographs taken by others add to the collection, not least because of my faulty memory.

I nearly wrote 'snapshuts'. For another picture comes to mind to indicate what happened that day towards the end of May three years ago. The house of my being was not secure against the elements, and too many windows were open. A stormy wind hurled me along a passage, and my foot dislodged the catch of a trapdoor that I did not know existed. I fell down rotten steps, the door clanged shut, and I landed unconscious on the stone floor of a dark cellar. There was enough air through a ventilation shaft for survival. From time to time voices and shadowy figures would impinge on my awareness, and they became clearer as my eyes got used to the dark. Some were earthed enough to sit with me without intruding and helped me discover that the stone floor was trustworthy. And little by little the steps were repaired with the help of 'angel-messengers' descending and ascending upon them. A few sat on the top step and blocked out the light ...

I

Turbulence

It was the only time you ever saw me. I had come to the surgery for a routine check-up and you were a student on placement, learning from the interaction between my doctor and those patients who gave permission for you to be there. Some intuition, perhaps from your own experience or from acute observation, made you wonder aloud after I had gone: he may be heading for a depression.

Months later, a number of you were puzzled about samples of my behaviour which were bizarre (at least more so than usual!) That's odd. Rather unlike Jim. But you had neither reason nor occasion to pool your temporary unease. 'If onlys' are useless, even if in retrospect we utter them. Could catastrophe have been prevented if you had thought to 'have a word in season' or had 'raised the alarm'? Perhaps my distress would have been less intense, but enough had been happening to lead to a crisis, unaware though I was of gathering storm clouds, some of which were as small as the child's hand which once upon a time had been unable to prevent the moisture forming.

There is a dark cloud surrounding my maternal grandfather, a man of uncertain temper and wandering eye. He had four daughters, two of whom have hinted to me of his cruelty. I have no reason to think it anything but sporadic, and do not know if what he did would now be called abusive. But his eldest daughter suffered from depression throughout her life, and ended that life by her own hand when in her seventies. What do we inherit genetically, and

I

what unresolved material from our ancestors' lives comes down to us, only to surface through the events and relationships of our own lives? I am convinced that no blame should be attached to those whose boat does *not* survive a squall.

It is years now since we have been in touch, but a memory has been nudged of the time we were in college together. You began to panic about your examinations and went home for a week or two to relieve the pressure. A couple of other friends were also showing signs of stress. Tension was building and I remember feeling that it was somehow 'infectious'. Who was going to be the next? It was the first time I experienced the desire to protect myself from those who might be mentally ill, to withdraw, to push away. Years later, I became a little familiar with one or two of those large hospitals built at the end of the last century, well beyond the city boundaries in what was then sparsely populated countryside, out of sight of London, Leeds, and the rest ...

As you got to know me, you became convinced that I had been depressed for years. Not that you were glib about using the word: the label might be convenient for describing a cluster of symptoms, but the syndrome is experienced in a unique way by each human being so afflicted. I shall never be able to pinpoint a cause, only factors, and triggers, and final straws.

I have never been comfortably at home in my flesh-body. Very early shocks, not least around birth, and susceptibility to illness in my early years, made me suspicious and watchful. Body contact was not always trustworthy and nurturing. And the white Anglo-Saxon Protestant culture of my childhood hardly helped to make good a deficit of healthy touch: we were never taught that particular grammar, hardly even the alphabet.

My grandparents did not approve of the man you fell in love with. They stifled your passion and you married for security a man whose even temper and patience were in marked contrast to your father's temperament. You then – unconsciously I think – transferred your passion on to your only son, especially after your second son did not survived infancy. You let me go into public life, ambitious for me there, but you were reluctant to let me be emotionally and sexually independent. Somewhere inside were you saying, "If I can't have you, nobody will"?

I find myself calm enough now as I write that. But thank you for the image of me in a loin cloth furiously fighting off the clinging Medusa – even for that of Ulysses strapped to the ship's mast, defiant against the Sirens who would tear him down. It has been vital to begin to exult in that kind of energy: no wonder 'bottling it up' was 'de-pressing'.

Throughout my early adult years, you sold me that dynamic as the 'cause' of my homosexual orientation. Another oversimplification of a complex phenomenon! I can see the connection between what happened early on, with my being out of touch with touch, and my adult difficulties in sustaining intimacy in a relationship. But I am uneasy about single explanations – like the one about weak fathers not bonding well with their sons. It was so easy to associate my adolescent struggles with my father, with his being weaker than my mother, thus selectively ignoring his strengths and the deep connections we had already made. Some of those have occurred to me alas only since his death.

Nevertheless, there may indeed be strands here which caused turbulence and also which made acceptance of my sexual identity difficult. Add to that the impressions made in a young man in the fifties and early sixties by the institutional messages that to be homosexual was at best sick (psychiatry), certainly sinful (church), and, for men, criminal (law). This is not the place for an analysis of oppression, enough to note that here was another half-hidden pressure. Op-press and de-press are allied words.

Our relationship changed – as all relationships change, and it changed in a unique way – as all such relationships change in a unique way. It is the uniqueness that makes them more painful. And it can appear that more change is happening for the one than for the other. It may not be so, but in any case such changes may make impossible (humanly speaking) the love that does not alter "when it alteration finds". Shakespeare kept me going for a while, as did Auden, who puts a definition of faith into the mouth of Joseph in his poem on the Nativity, *For the Time Being*: "to choose what is difficult all one's life as if it were easy, that is faith." But the strain can be too great.

Changes towards greater truth about ourselves are always liberating. We shed yet another persona, a mask, an actor's part. But it can be bewildering to those who have not before seen beyond – and much more painful than meeting an actor in the bar after the performance.

I have a number of friends who are gay, but who are or have been married. Much more has been 're-orientated' (at least temporarily) than sexual intercourse. Social intercourse changes too. Neighbours, colleagues, friends (even gay friends) relate to a married couple. There are shifts, often subtle, in topics and style of conversation. Connections with the gay world thin and vanish. This may or may not be important to one whose way of life changes, but it happens, and it is bound to have an effect – damaging if the change is denying a fundamental truth about one's being. To allow oneself to be twisted out of true is one definition of 'sin' – not a realization to make you feel worthless and wracked with guilt, but again an entanglement, a pressure, in which it is all too easy to be caught and which can help lead to the contradictions that eventually produce crisis. And it is hard to give up the pretence when society and church smile with approval.

❖

I thought I knew Shakespeare's *Hamlet* very well. I studied it for 'A' level English Literature and even enjoyed learning the recommended quotations off by heart. I have seen at least half a dozen productions on the stage. But seeing Kenneth Branagh's film recently alerted me to a dimension of the story I had known with my head but now recognized through my heart's recall of the summer of 1991.

Three of the characters in *Hamlet* suffer a double bereavement. Laertes returns from Paris to a murdered father and a sister unhinged and drowned, and he reacts with wild anger. That sister is Ophelia, driven to despair and suicide by her father murdered by her beloved Hamlet, who in turn has rejected her. Hamlet himself, dangerously flirting with madness, is told that his father was poisoned by his uncle, and, instrumental in Ophelia's madness, suffers the loss of her as well.

Any major loss can push us into wild vengeful grief, or can turn the anger inwards in self-destruction. When two such bereavements happen within weeks, it is hard to prevent the one being locked into the other, and the necessary process of grieving each is frustrated by confusion, shock, and muddle. The toxins which need to be discharged through anger and tears accumulate in the organism, to later greater distress.

Add to that another broad brush stroke: a character

who needs to be in control (or at least in control of the
occasional, well structured, giving up of control!) No
wonder that the crisis, when it came, was dramatic. A complicated Gordian knot had tightened: too many threads had
become entangled and could not be used to weave a distinctive pattern.

Because of my lack of a comfortable sense of being embodied, and because of a stigmatized sexuality, I have rarely had
a clear and balanced sense of my own worth. Thus it has
been a constant surprise to me to receive affirmation for
what I do and am. Add to this an ability to weave magic with
words, and nomadic work which rarely gives others an opportunity to see me behind the stage (or pulpit or altar), and
I am set up for – and I set myself up for – admiration,
pedestals, and isolation, none of which is good for me or for
anyone else. Neither did a solitary childhood and a clumsy
fear of team sports help. It may be marvellous (it is) to have
friends all over the world, but nomads in crisis need more
connections than by telephone. Networks are all very well,
but they are disembodied. And I have never been a 'local'
person, content with neighbourhoods, gossip, and the
evening paper. Not that I am without compassionate and
practical neighbours, nor above a bit of gossip, but I am
usually the one who is either arriving or departing.

I have never been attracted to mathematics, philosophy,
or chess. If I am a thinker, it is through intuition and
imagination rather than logic. But I find it hard to switch
off from the process of sifting, discerning, linking, and
re-shaping whatever material comes my way. Even when
I idle (in bath and along beach), something new will often
occur to me: life seems full of small 'eureka' moments. (I
was using a strimmer yesterday, and this morning I notice
a sheep making a more efficient job of cropping the grass

around a rock. A new image for a poem? No copyright.)

Now this can be fun. But it can also be too much. For a wordsmith alive today has to – or at least this one feels called (bound, compelled, required) to – digest the accumulated awfulness of the story of his parents' generation, all that is brought to light and symbolized by the Somme, Auschwitz and Hiroshima. Along with that is my own generation's opportunity to question and begin to live alternatives to inherited, often damaging, ways of living our human sexuality.

To write and speak of these things is in itself risky because of the necessary exposure to what is negative in the world. It is hard, but vital, for me to admit that I have done these things without sufficient grounding in a greater love and truth ('God') or sufficiently realistic dependence on the nurturing oases of protective places and people.

For years I have taken for granted as normal the amount of energy needed to swim against the current in polluted waters. I foolishly had not counted the cost.

I was full to bursting with accumulated stuff. (And still there are those fascinating people to meet and books to buy and – one day – read …) My work was on overdrive (partly in compensation for the bereavements), allowing others space, keeping the boundaries for them, and neglecting my own needs.

You put it well: I ingest too much, certainly emotionally and mentally, and probably physically (looking at the scales in these late convalescent days). Do I digest, assimilate, and eliminate in due proportion? There is too much clutter, not enough letting go. (Why is the sheer pleasure of a healthy bowel movement unmentionable? Perhaps wealthy countries are suffering under the weight of the cumulative constipation of too many possessions – and thoughts, and books, including this one …)

What I went through is barely hinted at by the diagnosis of 'severe reactive depression'. It can happen to those who are at least one layer short on protective 'skin', who have endured a fractured infancy, who are open-minded and openhearted, and who ingest too much.

And did I pick up something else in the air that was toxic? You pointed out to me that I live on the edge of a 'depressed' inner city. There is calm in my house, there is the green of birch and sycamore and oak outside my window, and there is beauty in the line of distant hills, but at my feet? And down the road? What is the connection between personal and corporate dis-ease? The palls of smoke may no longer hang over the city, flecks of black falling on clothes drying in the sun, but there is something invisibly polluting that hangs heavily over us. Is it too fanciful to think that here was one more factor to increase the likelihood of crisis? I think it was the Australian poet Les Murray who opined that depression is the key to modern thought and politics.

You were too dependent on me, victim to my rescuer who happily colluded. So you drained me of energy, and I was too unaware to plug the leaks. And that was paralleled by my choosing to buy a large corner house lifted up from the road in front, its appearance a pleasing gift to passers-by, its garden largely visible to the public eye, some of its privacies compromised, its offerings easily devoured, leaving an emptiness within.

It was strange (and providential?) that your exploration of

stress as experienced by professional carers should have given you that unexpected case study that was myself – a gift I would prefer not to have been able to proffer!

You wrote of the top level of stress, ordinary mistakes that we learn, from painful but not damaging experience. This is the area of that boring sensible advice about diet and exercise; habits that might, unwatched, become compulsions; sleep and relaxation; holidays and keeping friendships in good repair. In that list, each of us has weak spots that need attention. Making holidays enjoyable? No to cream teas? Finding ways of physically moving that are enjoyable and not drudgery? The caps fit.

The next level is unavoidable if we are living at all sensitively in a rapidly changing world. I have indicated some of that stress already. Of course it comes along with the personal stress that is presented by client to carer. How much burden-bearing is it prudent to undergo? Again, I now see myself more clearly.

It is the third level that you rightly discern as the most complex and damaging, stress that precipitates a precipitous cliff fall which may result in an injury from which there can be no recovery. Indeed – this is to anticipate – I nearly died, and, I suspect, in less skilful and gentle hands, might well have found myself in an institution for life. I am almost certain that that would have been the case fifty years ago. (Who was behind the walls I fearfully passed as a young child in the forties?)

You write of hidden forces, distorting, disrupting, erupting into 'attacks' on the heart and brain. I had neglected the cellar of my being, had not asked sufficiently or often enough for a companion to come down the steps with me, torch strapped to a head and heart that would help to shine light in dark neglected corners. O the irony – I have spoken and written of these things, deluding myself and others that I knew more about them than I do: the controller pretends to have it all sorted. Perhaps at the level of the organizing mind there is indeed clarity. But the consequence is all the more painful for those hidden parts of me that were ignored, and, in some way or other, however obscure the code, insist on being heard. Because the encounter with such hidden truth is painful, I shy away, blind to a reality that is clear to everyone else, or I project my unexamined troubles on to others, *my* film appearing on *their* screen and obscuring the picture they are trying to describe.

No wonder that blind unthinking rage boils up to explode through the heavy rocks of accumulated depressing, dead – and deadly – weight. And the despair which is its neighbour.

The week before I 'broke down' I became manic. I rang you to say I had been travelling from the depths of hell to the gates of heaven. I remember a careful and lucid car journey across Sheffield when everything that happened seemed full of meaning for my future. I had a detailed vision for the Church, convinced I could embody it in one particular parish. None of it was irrational, but the ideas were exploding like firecrackers.

(When I shared them with you, though, I was out of touch with the job you had a right to expect from me, that *I* would be listening to *you*. I am not surprised now that you felt dazed and irritated.)

I scribbled a lot that week, not in any ordered way, but on scraps of paper, whatever was to hand, lest I should lose track of even the smallest detail. My handwriting, never brilliant, deteriorated rapidly.

I also began to lose touch with other boundaries: I spent a lot of money on Barclaycard that week. One evening when the house was empty, I went to the chapel on the top floor, and without my usual inhibitions, opened heart and lungs to sing the hymn, *Thine be the Glory*. A resurrection theme matched my mood and expressed my conviction. My scribbling reminds me that I sang rather than shouted. I'm not so sure now; in any case, it was all too intense to last, and I was losing my grip on any ladder by which I could safely return to the ground.

The last coherent entry in my journal was for a Wednesday in the middle of May. (A week later I was in hospital.) Part of it is a description of how everything seemed to be *flowing*, especially the everyday things like chores and neighbourly exchanges in shops and city centre – I recorded nine of them. A new slipway off the inner ring road led me 'astray' and I found myself in the recently opened car park of a new branch of 'Safeway'. It was lunch time and I bought a huge helping of lasagne, chips and beans – and a bottle of mineral water – not my usual fare but typical of an occasional downmarket blow-out! I reached over to another table for some adverts for the Daily Mirror which were blank on the back, and I wrote five Statements, two of which are more appropriate towards the end of this book, under *Breezes*, but here verbatim are the first three:

I *know* what a psychotic breakdown is, why you can flip if too much material surfaces too quickly without sufficient rooted connection to the ground, physical health, and ego strength. The many waters *do* then *drown* love, contrary to the opposite moment of exultation recorded in the Song of Songs. It is my own precise fear of course.

I *know* how prolific writers get their material. I am super aware of detail a hundred times more than usual.

I *know* how closely psychosis is linked with creativity, why madness is never far from the creative writer.

That knowledge was more than surface: it was gut knowledge, soul-deep. But it did not stop my falling into that terrifying place, for an awful, dreadful six months and a further very bleak year. I went awry, from the disturbance of the cells of my brain to a lack of connection with my closest friends and with those other cherished companions, words.

As I write this three years later, I am comforted by warm sunny June weather, looking out on a calm sea and the irregular but stable outline of the mountains of Torridon. But my next task is to describe the squall and its immediate aftermath. It will not be easy.

Strangely, I nearly forgot the very last coherent entry in my journal, two days later. It is full of bitter irony, and I can but hope that it may yet come true in an embodied and lived way, sobered as I am by all that has happened since:

I have come through a great tribulation in this spring of 1994, the worst of times and the best of times. At last coming into my own, publicly and personally, that terrible split being healed.

The years that the locusts have eaten have been restored.

Not yet, not yet. The in-sights, the in-scape, may be in place. But I cannot make them part of my land-scape. They are too many to ground. It is not only the lightning flash of pain that is hard to earth: even more the joy.

Not yet the integration.

Now comes the dis-integrating.

And I dreamed a dream. My mother and I are in the same room doing separate jobs, I do not know what she is doing. I am writing notes on various bits of paper. She asks me to join her, I say, not till I've finished. She asks again. No, I need to finish this job first ... A large furry brown spider is scuttling around the room, but it is not approaching either of us.

II

Squall

The roundabout was spinning faster and faster. I held on as long as I could – a long time. So the fall was far worse than it might have been, and the recovery took longer too.

Another picture. The trigger was pressed. I shot into the air – very high – as from the barrel of a gun. The descent was swift and sudden. I hit the ground, and bounced a few times down a slope. I eventually hit bottom, fell into a river unconscious – and almost died. I was stimulated by shock into movement out of an almost catatonic state. Very, very, very slowly I moved upwards again.

No wonder in those weeks before I fell you saw me trapped, fists clenched, tensed, wound up like a spring, unable to release the anger which had built up. And when it came, I imploded rather than exploded. The anger stretched back a long way, focused from time to time on parents and churches (especially the uniformed branch), and on particular people, including the triggers, no more nor less significant than others over the years, but the ones who happened to be there when the pressure had built up to the intolerable. Expressing anger appropriately – in context and in proportion – had never been modelled to me as I grew up. Without realizing it, I had imbibed the depressed culture of the churches, where you must never admit to being angry and never express it. But of course what is unexpressed grows inside, and once in a while, unaware and unseeing, it fires its shot.

❖

13

Whitesquall was not a very good film, despite the good looks of the young American hunks who were probably the main reason for my being drawn to a holiday evening's entertainment on the Isle of Man a year or so ago now. But the sequence depicting the squall itself was gripping. Its destructive force made you almost smell the fear.

I looked up the origins of the word 'squall': 'squeal' is there (the fear) and 'bawl' (the anger and the grief). Behind 'bawl' may be the medieval Latin 'baulare', to bark, and the Icelandic 'baula', to low, like an ox. (No wonder the baby awoke – and I'm not just thinking of the Christmas hymn – when the cattle started lowing!)

I could add other associated words. Their sound more than vividly conveys meaning: howl, screech, bellow, keen, shriek, roar ...

And when the squall hit the coast, the new born lambs were hurled against the wire fence, stunned and sliced to death ...

Neurotics build castles in the air; psychotics live in them; psychiatrists charge the rent.

❖

Well, the medical record certainly indicates a psychotic episode. Baudelaire once wrote; "I have felt the wind of the wing of madness." And indeed I was temporarily mad, 'insane', out of my mind, 'elsewhere' to those who looked on, stood by, or took responsibility.

❖

I have no memory of the twenty-four hours or so after I slipped. I had put my cycle on the train to spend a few days with solid friends. I cycled the last twenty miles of the journey and arrived at your house, tense and tired but showing no unusual symptoms. I can recall some conversation but not a a great deal. I remember being 'high' the next day, sitting by the river and speaking into a small tape recorder ...

You became more aware and concerned at my cascading thoughts, too many, too quickly. At first I was coherent, but later I disintegrated from sentences to staccato phrases, to isolated words, to babble – akin to 'speaking in tongues', but the kind that do *not* build up in love, but merely make the separation and the isolation worse. The tools of my trade had shattered: the wordsmith, who would have been wise to linger longer in chosen silence, had been utterly silenced ...

You write to me of the gift I have for communication, of my quick, complex, and subtle mind, of my lively wit and humour. When you phoned me in hospital, I was slow to react (if indeed I reacted at all), my thought processes were confused, and when I spoke it was hesitantly, sometimes with slurred speech ...

You welcomed me into your kitchen, and I began to behave strangely. I spoke wildly, not making sense. I began to jump about and at one point fell to the ground. A macabre dance indeed ...

I confronted you in the middle of the night and was unrecognizable. I was paranoid, thinking myself under attack by people who wanted to kill me. I was insistent that you call my bank manager immediately to take some secret material I was carrying into the vaults. I was desperately afraid, I clung to you, and you were seriously alarmed that I might attack you. It took you over an hour to calm me down. I 'returned to myself', tired and sleepy. In the morning I appeared to be reasonably normal, though unaware of my bizarre behaviour during the night. But it was not too long before I slipped more deeply into a psychotic state, in which I might at any moment have acted violently, against you or against myself.

You were then wisely instrumental in moving me from the personal world to the professional. With the protective power of the Mental Health Act, and the actions of local doctor and police, I was taken to hospital, where some hours later I 'came to' to discover from the form on the bedside locker that I had been sectioned. I was disorientated, subdued, washed out, withdrawing into the long tunnel which I was for months to inhabit ...

And, as the first of many acts of friendship in those months, you rushed to see me, collecting a speeding ticket on the way ...

Last year I saw a news item on television that estimated there were three to six million unexploded landmines in Bosnia. And what of Afghanistan, Cambodia, and the rest? Of course, for any one human being, the one that explodes in your face is the one you remember, and not all the wounds heal ...

This parallel may help. Suppose you have been in a bad traffic accident and have undergone major surgery. You have been in and out of 'intensive care'. You need medication to prevent relapses. You need to be in 'maximum security'. Your return to health will be very gradual, and you will need a long convalescence.

Here is a summary of the medical interventions:

I was given haloperidol twice, an anti-psychotic drug, once towards the end of May 1994, and again in the middle of June. Later, and continuously from mid-July 1994 to mid-May 1995, I was given a milder anti-psychotic drug, sulpiride.

Between the middle of June and the end of August 1994 I was regularly taking the anti-depressive drug amitriptylene, 75 mg at first, and then 150 mg.

I was prescribed lorazepam, a sleeping pill, as and when needed; as time went on, the dosage was gradually reduced.

Replacing the amitriptylene, which appeared to be having little effect, was fluoxitene, more commonly known as prozac. I took this regularly from September 1994, very gradually reducing the dosage in the early months of 1996, finally coming off it in May of that year.

There were two further crises following the initial collapse towards the end of May 1994, as a result of which I was given electro-convulsive therapy, five times between 15 and 29 July, four times between 9 and 19 September.

The only side effects of the drugs of which I am aware is that the sulpiride made me continuously anxious and restless, though thankfully I was able to sleep, and I did not need to take a sleeping pill on more than a few occasions. It is of course impossible to know if any or all of the drugs prevented anything worse happening, nor whether they will have any long-term effects. (And it is characteristic of me to want to know, and so be in at least partial control.)

A well-documented side effect of ECT is short-term memory loss. I am certainly hazy about all that was going on in that summer of 1994. But I was giving up the will to live, and there came a point when ECT was the only action left. I had stopped caring for myself, but I was able to fool staff and visitors that I was still eating and drinking when in

fact I had stopped doing so and had become seriously de-
hydrated.

At this point I became a medical oddity. I had been given
a blood test which showed that I might have had a tumour.
It was vital to do a brain scan (using CT, or computerised to-
mography) before risking ECT, but the ECT itself was by
that time urgent. The decision was taken to give the shock
treatment in the scanning room, once the scan itself had
shown there was no tumour. However, because I was so
restless, I could not sit still long enough for the scan to be
taken. So I was given a general anaesthetic, under which I
received both scan and ECT. This was high drama, worthy
of television soap. A nurse ran along a corridor with the
ECT equipment precariously balanced on a trolley, while a
second anaesthetist was summoned when the first was called
away by his bleep on an even more urgent mission. I of
course was blissfully (well, hardly) unaware.

The second course of ECT was given because I deteriorated yet again. I spent much of the time on the floor of a
side room of the ward, almost totally uncommunicative. I
am not sure if it was on this or the first occasion that I was
transferred for a night to a general ward as a medical emergency, but I am told that on that occasion I screamed and
raged the night through. I am sure that this was something
I needed to do, and I am glad I was not sedated out of it –
though I owe an apology to the other patients for what must
have been a disturbed night.

Well, ECT worked. It re-established certain rhythms or
patterns or waves in my brain, and from the September onwards I did very slowly begin to improve. I can still remember the door into the euphemistically labelled 'Treatment
Suite', the brown knobs on the chairs in the waiting room,
the step up to a couch, the slight prick of the needle, and the
cup of tea and biscuit afterwards. There were nine occasions
but only one coalesced memory.

The memory makes me cringe still. But I realize that the
treatment can be a *mercy*. Nobody knows why it works or

why it sometimes does not. While it is not now used as a routine procedure, it is in extremis. Without it, I might very well not have been alive to tell the tale. I was nearly totally overpowered by the accumulated distress: I very nearly didn't pull through.

You knew I was physically healthy, my heart was sound, but how much more could my organism take? ... And at the other extreme, you saw a stooped old man in geriatric care, with glazed eyes, needing a baby sitter in his second childhood.

So much for the drama. But most of the time on an admission ward of a psychiatric hospital life was humdrum. You had worked for twenty years in a number of such hospitals and when you first visited me you found it familiar and reassuring. You were relieved to observe the quality of the care I was receiving, so often downgraded and perceived as unglamorous. Basic team medical psychiatry was doing its job, and doing it well. It gave me space, structure, security, patience, kindness, and necessary treatment. Fashions come and go, but the basic core is trustworthy.

Inevitably, some of my fleeting memories are less flattering. Psychiatric and geriatric wards are the poor relations of the health service and do not attract the resources given to high-tech glamorous medicine. The ward needed decorating and brightening up – I can still see the peeling wallpaper. (Visiting me on three successive days, you noticed the same sandwich on the floor in a corner all its own.) I never had the discussion I would have liked with a nutritionist about diet, and I still do not know whether to believe the story that hot meals had been cooked in another city, brought here by road, and simply reheated before serving. I was disturbed by the changes of staff, especially those who did odd shifts as irregulars: they seemed little more than minders. And however life-saving ECT was for me, will other procedures yet to be devised make it seem barbaric a hundred years from now?

It still feels awful that the ward felt more secure than home, which I could see from the hospital grounds a minute's walk away. But it was, so terrifying had the ordinary become. On one occasion an uncontrollable trembling stopped only when I was back in nursing hands. Later, when I was spending some nights at home, and some on the ward each week, I remember coming back to the hospital to find my expected bed occupied by another patient. I was just about coping well enough by then to return by taxi to sleep a further night at home.

I can only be profoundly thankful that for one or two people the ward became familiar territory because you visited me so frequently. It was that frequency and regularity (not *length* of visit) that counted, making me feel less insecure. But at first it was confusing for you: without uniform, staff were not obviously distinct from patients. And sometimes you had to use a different entrance because the doors were guarded against disruption from 'increased ward activity' (another euphemism).

Those regular telephone calls helped too, though the phone was often answered by other patients, who would variously say that I wasn't there, or that I had gone home, or that there was no such person. And if they said they would look for me, as often as not the phone was left dangling and no one came. Isolation and dislocation were an everyday part of life on the ward.

So I have few memories of my fellow patients, indeed few other memories at all. Just one or two further snapshuts [sic!] from what was hardly even a macabre holiday: the ghetto blaster from behind a curtain opposite, sometimes at full volume and its owner nowhere to be seen; the old door lock to the side room I slept in for a while, whose key had not been used in years: the keyhole was on the outside, which did not help me to feel less paranoid; and a nasty moment when I hallucinated, convinced that the smoke alarm in the ceiling was really a conduit for poison gas.

Mostly, dull routine – meals, tea breaks avoiding tobacco smoke, lying on my bed staring into space, pacing up and down the corridor, anxiety and occasional panic; fitful resting ...

Moods shifted. There were times of lucidity amid the storm and stress, even if I have no memory of them. I wrote to you in one such lull soon after my admission to hospital, saying that I feared it would be a long haul. I did wonder if it would ever end, echoing King Lear's chilling words, "Never, never, never, never, never." To that, those of you who had accompanied others through their darkness, replied, "You will come through. You will come through."

You saw me oscillate between times of relative 'normality', subdued but coherent, reflecting on what was happening to me, and times when I was easily excitable (even wickedly childlike) or acutely anxious, or, most frightening of all, prostrate and totally cut off from you and my surroundings. And reminders of my unresolved grief would set off a mood of agitation and distress.

At times in those early weeks I would try and convince others and myself that I was not as ill as I really was. The

medical staff were sometimes reluctant for me to be at
home, but I could be very persuasive. After all, I said one
afternoon, I had my resident chaplain to look after me!

You took me out on a beautiful summer evening for a drive
in the Peak District, finishing with a meal in a restaurant
where I ordered and paid for the most expensive wine. On
returning home I played some of my favourite music. You
went to bed and I stayed up most of the night, again very
high. By the following evening the anxieties and irrational
fears returned. You called an ally. By the time he arrived, I
was afraid to be in the house, and he kept me company as I
paced round the garden for a long time. Eventually he took
me to his home, where his wife was remarkably unfazed and
welcoming. But I was far too anxious and insecure to settle,
and I do have a memory of talking wildly outside the hospital entrance as he sought my readmission in the early
hours of the morning. For the next two days I was heavily
sedated.

On another occasion quite early on, I persuaded the two of
you to accompany me home for the afternoon. I wanted to
rearrange some furniture and move some books, seeking to
create a cross between a den and a sanctuary in a couple of
rooms on the second floor of my house. I wanted somewhere that I could guard against all intrusion. But of course
I was far from being content and calm enough to inhabit
them and feel secure. Hospital was the only safe place, confused as I was and unable at that time to accept the fact.

I suppose the most dramatic contrast is the one I am least
aware of now, simply because of the memory loss associated
with ECT. From being unaware, not communicating, occasionally crying out, dehydrating, a medical emergency who

might not see the morning, to that very next morning sitting up in bed, tired but cheerful, and greeting you when you came, full of trepidation, to visit.

Then more ordinary moods – you remember walking with me round the hospital grounds, prising me out of the ward to take me for a pub lunch, and sitting in the passenger seat of my car, your hand hovering over the handbrake as I drove a few hundred yards for the first time since falling ill. The parallel strikes me as accurate when you think of the first steps after a severe physical illness is past its worst crises.

Fitfully, I kept a diary in hospital. One of the medical staff's concerns was that I should try and learn to *manage* my anxiety, and I have a record of some of this.

> Stop. Breathe. Breathe gently. Breathe down and out.
>
> The next tablet is coming by 10 pm.
>
> *Try* and panic. Ha! You can't!
>
> Think through the worst scenarios from last time you were anxious which haven't actually happened: "I won't survive the night … Nobody will believe me … I will be dead in a few minutes … I will never get back home … I have become one of the walking dead, aware of my surroundings but unable to move …"
>
> Split the anxieties into smaller more easily manageable bits.

In the days immediately before the worst crisis, I was increasingly afraid. I was *aware* of the fear rather than able to *feel* it. It was as if terror itself, almost an alien power, was slowly anaesthetizing me and draining me of my will to live. Even a visit and a phone call from two of the most perceptive people I know failed either to reassure or to reach the fear ...

I wake up full of fear after a fitful night's sleep. It is much harder to manage fear than it is to manage anxiety ... Another visitor ... and I feel more calm ... But the controlling optimistic me still tries to deceive that I am all right really ... No, I *am very ill*: this is no mere midlife crisis ... Forgive me, I have kept up appearances too much, but I cannot hide here: this ward is a very honest place ... I feel I have protected my vulnerable loving self with too much clutter, with a degree of wealth beyond most of the world's dreams ... Have I built too many barns for more storage? Will this night my soul be required of me? I am stripped to nothing: is there really a love and life beyond the mask of terror which seems to be all there is? ... Can I live *through* the fear? ... Will I ever work again? ... Will I ever travel again, or am I bound for life to this strip of land, hospital at one end, home at the other? The thought of bus, train, or plane, or anywhere beyond this city, is intolerable.

So the brainsquall continued, now furiously, now with an apparent easing of the fury. It lasted four months before the winds began finally to subside. But mine was not the only squall, or if it was, a great number of other people were caught up in it.

Rumours abounded. I had suddenly developed fullblown AIDS, or I was terminally ill with cancer. It was too horrible to talk about. Some people found themselves unable simply to say, 'a bad breakdown and severe depression'. However inadequate those words at least they are a clear signpost. So many people tried to find out. The hospital switchboard was inundated with enquiries, so much so that they pleaded for something to be done. It was, they said, like having a pop star in the hospital. (I can't bring myself to say which one, but it's not a comparison I particularly relish!)

Too many visitors began to turn up, some anxious to do something rather than simply to be a comforting silent presence.

I was raising too many anxieties in others. One of you, thankfully beyond that kind of reaction, made it all the more ordinary by saying that what had happened to me could happen to anyone. I suspect that this was precisely the point. If this can happen to *anyone*, it could happen to you, or you, or you ... None of us is immune ... And that thought made some people panic ...

So you were angry with me too, for reminding you that you are vulnerable and mortal. Those of you who were dependent on my being around for you were suddenly bereft. You were seeking reassurance that everything would soon be resolved, that my normal service to you would be resumed. For others of you, what had happened was so awful and frightening that you could make no move in my direction at all: you withdrew, unable to keep 'in touch' ...

How could I do this to you? Me, of all people, one of the most together people you knew – or thought you knew. You wanted to shake me angrily and ask me how I could have been so unaware of what was building up. But you also knew that these 'things' accumulate slowly, and all of us think we are on top of the situation (perilously of course, because when we are on top, it can be a long way down). An otherwise unremarkable pebble is all that is needed to start an avalanche. You didn't reason that out at the time of course: you were in shock, disturbed, disorientated, feeling like a

refugee in exile from the safety and vitality I had habitually
given you. And I needed you to be a sanctuary for me. No
wonder you felt anger – and guilt that you could not do
much to help ...

Genial giant, more familiar than most with what was going
on, you were a centre of calm for many of those hurled
about by the squall. You interpreted for those who were bewildered. You tried to put some structure around their confusion. You asked people to give me space and not to hurry
me along ...

And you, loyal and determined, who could easily be writing
the alternative, perhaps more scurrilous, version of these
events, kept the externals of my life going. You kept anxious
visitors at bay, organized (with the help of some and despite
the hindrance of others) mundane matters of finance and
administration, fending off demands for payment and coping with a whirlwind of an author, however minor and temporary the meteorological phenomenon compared with my
own. How you did it all I shall never know, nor shall I ever
know everything that you did ...

And you, close by, who helped at one remove – a shoulder,
a cup of tea (or was it something stronger?) a laugh, an ear,
a mowing of the lawn to save me from having to face yet
one more anxiety when I came home ...

In the end, enough links held, enough connections were
made, to prevent utter and complete disaster.

The medical staff – three of them in particular – kept on
believing in me, did not give up inside and retreat into
mechanical routines. There was something alive enough in

me for them not to give up hope, even when there was no apparent contact ...

You said that you did not spend as much time with me as you would have liked. You were going through a period of fresh adjustment and assessment in your personal and professional life. Nevertheless, the will to communicate never left you. If it had, I think I would have recognized it, to my own deep despair. You kept me from that – as did you, who knew that it was vital to keep regular and frequent contact even when there was no apparent response ...

Then there were those links you made behind the scenes where my public life was concerned, keeping some in good repair, making new ones where necessary, tapping financial resources, supporting others who were helping to keep home and business going. And all those telephone calls many of you were making, to support me and one another, to clarify confusions, to get the most accurate help when needed. I shudder to think what the total bill amounted to, but it was to British Telecom's profits and to my well-being and gratitude – as to those who organized a kind of 'Easter Collection' for the 'Vicar', unbeknown to me for months until I began to take an interest in bank statements again ...

Some links were more dramatic and direct. You write of my violent rocking in my chair, crying, shaking, terrified, grabbing your arm, clinging on and bruising you. You had the courage to stay calm; you did not leap backwards through your own anger and fear. You risked treading on thin ice; each time you visited, you never knew if you would find me irrational, frustrated, strange, or the person you knew, however frightened and subdued ...

You both came from a distance when you were able, confused about what you had heard, apprehensive as to what you would find, feeling guilty that you were not able to do more. What will we say? What will we be able to talk about? What state will he be in? In the event, you took me out for a pub lunch. I could acknowledge you, but I could not put anything into the exchange. You initiated ordinary conversation, and I remained very quiet. But you had come; you had kept in touch. And you visited me again some months later. Again we went out for a meal. We managed a short walk, and we all remembered that I had eaten an enormous amount! I was still apt to be anxious, agitated and upset when you were late arriving, grumpy that you needed to use the loo before we went out for lunch. Even that strengthened the link ...

Thank you for being honest about how difficult, no, how frightening it was to visit me. There is nothing that the visitor to the patient can *do*. Even the pastoral actions of prayer, of giving communion, even of touch, may have no visible effect. They do not appear to be doing any good, and they give no encouragement to the pastor. You found yourself wanting to get away quickly, away from a place which seemed so empty, from a person who seemed but a shell. A friendship that had been two-way had no substance any more because there was no response. You mentioned to me that you had been seeing a young man who said, "My soul has gone: I am only a shell." Simply to be with such a person, to be fully there, aware and alive, entering that empty nothing even for a few minutes, is terrifying, however rational we may be in talking about it. I am reminded of someone else's comment, "You had left us; and I did not know if you were coming back." Nevertheless, *you* came back, returning again and again despite your fear. But no wonder in such circumstances that the patient becomes suicidal, whether actively so with wrist-slashing, or passively so, as I did, simply giving up. If there is nothing here of me but a shell, there is no point in keeping a shell in existence, barely alive and not in any way that has meaning. *Yet you did not give up.* You did return, trusting that in time I would also return. And eventually we discovered that it was so, your remarking that my openness about my treatment, my helplessness, my feeling of guilt, had helped, as had my courage in fighting (too strong a word, crawling perhaps) my way back, despite the setbacks and falls ...

Ruggedly you believed in me too. Somehow, strangely, you had no anxiety about my basic mental health. Your intuition was that this episode of my life, however distressing and prolonged, was necessary, and that I would come through. That tenacious belief, I believe 'came across' to me, and I made contact with it, and it helped, however unaware of it I was at the time ...

You came to a house that was empty, apart from a few remembrances of times past. Each visit was a costly act of faith. Eventually he may return. You came in naked prayer, sometimes walking alongside the faded hulk in silence, sometimes simply pretending I was really there. Some days you thought you caught a faint echo of the person who used to live here. Sometimes you arrived with others in a kind of search party. Is he on his way back? What will he have salvaged from the journey? What wisdom thrown up by the billows from the hidden depths?

But it feels as if I have no pearls of great price. I return with no strange spices from the exotic orient. Didn't you realise? I was in the cellar all the time ...

You came to visit me that day, terrible for you, forgotten by me, where all that I communicated was utter despair. But

you came; and you didn't flee; and you returned, again and
again. You found me lying flat on my bed in my pyjamas, ex-
pressionless, staring at the ceiling, at first not moving at all,
then shaking involuntarily. I gazed at you, revealing the terrified face and body language of a rabbit helplessly cornered
and trapped. You offered what you could of empathy, sharing a little of my bewilderment and desperation, until I simply said, "I think you should go and leave me to bear this
alone."

Reluctantly, you made one of the most difficult and
painful exits you can remember ever having to make. For
three hours you lost yourself in – of all improbable places –
the anonymity of Europe's largest shopping mall.
Impersonal, lacking in beauty, it seemed to reflect the
empty, hopeless place of my abandonment, which on that
bleak sunny summer day began to cut into the dark and
lonely parts of you. Trying inadequately to cope, you drank
two pints of Wards Ale in a tasteless pub and wrote a letter
of concern to a mutual friend. You booked an air ticket for
a trip you were about to make, and you bought a pair of
shoes. What else was there to do? My isolation, my desolation, seemed beyond your reach.

But for all the four thousand miles you had to put between us, you did not desert me. The link held – and now,
its having come through that ever so testing crucible, it has
been forged stronger than ever.

Even the image of the cellar seems friendlier now. I was certainly trapped by that trap door that tripped me up. But
there was no malicious jailer actually imprisoning me. No
one ever slammed the bolts across. I may have been sectioned three times, prevented for my own and other people's safety from going out of the front door, but I was never
left on my own for long. And the cellar was mine, a safe,
protected place, and others patrolled the hallway above to
keep most of the hostile footsteps at bay. Perhaps my

deepest truer self had to make this desperate move: there was nothing left but to enforce a prolonged time out of too harsh and clear a light. And some things do grow in dark places: a range of fungi now brought up the steps. (Take care, though, at what I may be offering: I am not sure I can completely discern yet between the wholesome and the poisonous, though I hope you can recognize the mushrooms – organic, of course.) Maybe also some growing bulbs, now ready for the sunlight – hyacinths, I hope. They even survived the occasional opening of the cupboard door by those who were anxious to bring light because they were unable to sit peacefully in the dark.

I am reminded of George Herbert's plant which returned to its roots in winter, dead on the surface, its life hidden away, the dark earth protecting it. I came across it as I was recovering, and rejoiced with the poet at the unexpected spring. It is the second stanza of *The Flower:*

> Who would have thought my shrivelled heart
> Could have recovered greenness? It was gone
> Quite underground; as flowers depart
> To see their mother-root, when they have blown;
> Where they together
> All the hard weather,
> Dead to the world, keep house unknown.

You told me that in the East I would have been secluded in a darkened room, its boundaries safe, given food to keep me alive, and adequate sanitation. It would have been thought the place, potentially at least, of new revelation, of a new way of thinking. I would not have been given drugs.

Who is it to say that would have made for an easier or shorter time? You rightly point out that the structure of our thinking governs what we deem 'normal', and what we label

'manic', 'eccentric', 'aberrant'. But are these the only inter-
pretations? There are levels of distress that Western medicine finds it hard to cope with. Indeed, truth is not amusing.
Yes, I disturbed many people, and was perhaps dangerous in
more ways than one.

In the end I guess such comparisons do not help us very
much – except to say that East and West need each other, in
approaches to healing as much as in approaches to faith.
Truth is Two-Eyed is the title of a book by the late John
Robinson. Few of us have both eyes open; all of us at times
shut both; and most of the time we keep open only one,
which is often itself short-sighted, with the other eye at best
the lazy one. What was it you said? As a Westerner among
westerners, I gravitated towards the pit of horrors. East-
erners levitate towards the extremes of light? Do we need
your light, and do you need the richer darker colours of the
spectrum that we may bring? ...

As I have reflected on the worst of these times, I have kept
returning to the theme of power. It seems to me that when
power is shared among human beings, when talents and
skills are used to serve others' well-being and the good of
the community, then we see something of love and justice
in action. Because we are imperfect beings, however, we
tend to exercise a love of power rather than the power of
love. By this I mean a power over others, an intrusive power
that claims everything for ourselves, at others' expense. In
between is the practice of protective power, which is not
necessarily unloving but can be dangerous. Under the law
of the land we give certain people, under carefully laid down
conditions, authority for the time being to exercise a power
that does intrude on others, curtailing their freedom because there is a risk that they will harm either others or
themselves or both.

There are those who act as gate-keepers in hospitals, who can admit and refuse 'admission', who can keep visitors at bay. There are powers of restraint which have to be used from time to time. There was that awful moment when I woke up to find that I had been 'sectioned', detained against my will. There were times when I was, probably with some reluctance, given more freedom of movement than was wise ...

There were 'interventions' that I did not have the power to refuse, so incapable had I become of making decisions for myself. I was unable to say No to a drug that would have the unpleasant side-effect of making me feel continuously anxious and restless.

You tell me that you made an intervention one day that was probably a mistake, anxious as you were to demonstrate that you could exercise your own power well. I was in the grip of a panic attack, groaning and unable to communicate. You felt a pressure to do something because of my visitors. You tried to get me to breathe deeply in order to calm me down. With hindsight you wondered if it would have been better simply to make me comfortable and to let the panic pass in its own time. Appearing to care may not accurately reflect actual care. Sometimes we *act* because we are afraid to *be*. How often do we intrude because of our own anxieties? ...

I was moved when you told me that you had become a professional in psychiatry precisely because it made fewer claims than other branches of medicine. It is more self-critical, more cautious in intervening, more aware of how little we know. Knowledge may indeed imply power, and it is all too easy to pretend to know more than we actually do ...

❖

You mentioned that you had been taught by one of two men who in turn had been apprenticed to the man who wrote the first major text book on psychiatry at the end of the nineteenth century. A hundred years on I was being treated, with skill and kindness, by the 'grandson' and 'great-grandson' of the founder of a new discipline. When I had recovered enough to appreciate the point, I was humbled by their modesty ...

You were cautious, too, about how much could be conveyed by the broad brush strokes of diagnosis. 'Depression' is little more than a convenient label to convey *some* information about a unique event that is being experienced in a unique way by a unique person. A disease is an interaction between two or more variables, and can thus be complex. No wonder that intervention can often be ham-fisted, and that it is tempting for a medical student to be drawn to the kind of surgery where a precise cut can have a precise, usually predictable, effect ...

It has taken me years to realize how much I like to be in control, exercising power. So when the controller collapsed, there was an immediate power vacuum. There was no one person to take charge, and people 'out there' reacted in a confusing variety of ways – all of course unbeknown to me at that time. You asked yourself many times, Who owns Jim? Who is claiming what? Who is organizing house and business, therapy and sanctuary? Who is meeting personal needs? I now know that in the external squall there were a lot of people talking about me, with both benign intent and unconscious motive. Who kept information to themselves, enjoying the privileged access? Who leaked confidential information? And what in any case were the boundaries between public and relatively private knowledge? Temptations and opportunities for gossip were legion. Again, this does not necessarily imply ill will, but the reality was a complex web of social relationships and interactions, with myself prone in the middle. Gradually, the picture became clear, but there was considerable confusion and embarrassment in the process. Again, who was exercising what kind of power, and what kind of love?

There were some who were concerned to protect me from intrusion, not only medical staff in hospital. They were the hasty builders of scaffolding around the storm-damaged house of my being. In shock themselves, often bewildered and disturbed, they found courage to act.

Were others tempted to take over? It is the perennial temptation of carers and rescuers in the dangerous work of coming close to the vulnerable person who has neither strength nor ability to deny access. At last! A way into the life of someone who, when well, is perceived to have the power of money, sexual attractiveness, charisma. For months there was the possibility of hangers-on and movers-in, ever so well-meaning mafias ...

You spent hours convincing people that my life did not need taking over, and you somehow found your way through meddle and muddle. You began to distinguish between predatory and nurturing clergy, between fan club who claimed intimate friendship and friends of tested worth, between protectors of institutional reputations and protectors of my well-being, between the wielders of knives and the binders of wounds ...

One of the tests of friendship was, I suspect, the degree to which you felt wretched and helpless, knowing you were at heart powerless and yet not acting in such a way as to cover that feeling with inappropriate interventions. You were aware of the dark chasm down which a visitor may fall. You were baffled again by the mystery I presented to you, for I was laying bare the inadequacy of your skills and the paucity of your resources – not least spiritual resources. I was reminding you painfully of your own helplessness and feelings of abandonment. You looked at me and saw yourself on some unpredicted future date. I gave you no welcome, no smile, simply a mask devoid of expression on which you could draw your own terror. Your attempts at conversation were like playing tennis with yourself. You went away with no sense of satisfaction at having brought relief, fearful that you had merely added to my burden. And because you could walk away and I could not, you felt superior, more powerful, and you felt wretched about it ...

I suspect the poster in my kitchen mocked you. "It often shows a fine command of language to say nothing." A painful twist of paradox that: laying on one side one's power so that the other person may discover his own. How very, very hard it is to sit where they sit, saying precisely nothing, at most making contact with a hand whose touch is the very opposite of intrusive. They sat for seven days in silence, so great was his misfortune ...

You wrote somewhere of how boundless (boundary-less as well as bounding, and even bouncy) activity on behalf of others can be abusive. We hijack other people's pain in order to make ourselves feel better ...

Back to my own paradoxes of power and powerlessness. As I learned more about the external squall I had provoked, I found it at first hard to believe that so much had been going on. Of course I had been too ill to be aware, but there was that deep niggle of self-abasement ('a-basement' a case of self – or other – inflicted 'en-cellaring'?): I am not important enough to others for there to be all this activity on my behalf.

Along with this, hiding from my need for help (I am not worth much, people won't be able to do me any good, I have to make my own way), I became quite adept at fooling at least some of the people some of the time that I was getting better, that I was not as ill as I really was. Even a medical team do not have eyes and ears twenty-four hours a day and can act only on what information they have been able to glean, surmise or intuit. And my pretending self, defending against the pain, in the end so exhausted that I had no resources left, was nevertheless adroit for quite a while. You thought I was more in charge than I actually was.

From another perspective, we have that classic dynamic which you pointed out to me, of the controlling guru, too isolated on his pedestal for his own good, in turn enjoying (half-consciously at best) creating dependency, dangerously hardly believing that others would want to beat a path to his door. I also now know, though often unable to spot it, that people hold back from a guru, a little afraid, more than a little shy. (Yet I myself do the same, dithering about whether and how to introduce myself to say thank you to a distanced 'hero' whose words have meant a lot to me.)

What a relief to be *friends*, with neither having unrealistic expectations of the other, mutually seeing each other's weaknesses and strengths, flaws and skills. A relief too when neither of us fancies the other. I think two of you spent a little while eyeing each other up, both of you fiercely and accurately protective of me, wondering if the other had the romantic claws out for me! You were able to cheer each other up with much laughter once you realized that neither of you was so inclined ...

It was sobering for you to find a friend who you had always thought cleverer and more articulate than you, in a state where all such comparisons were irrelevant. What is that friendship now? What is it when we can no longer walk and talk and drink wine together? Yet on emerging together from this 'levelling' place, our friendship has deepened, has touched a level beyond that of the common interests which established the friendship in the first place. We have reached a more powerfully loving exchange, and the potential for new moments of contentment together, as yet unknown.

We are not in this world always to be happy, or even continuously content. We are not here with the expectation that we should *know* one another (and so have power *over* one another). We are here to learn that we are often wrong, always partial and incomplete in who we are and what we do. Perhaps we may grow a little – a little compassion, a little kindness, a little mercy, a grain of truth. Perhaps we may bear – and be scorched by – a few of the beams of love.

It was a power struggle. I had to separate myself and continue on my own life's path – as that dream of my mother showed. I could not give myself whole and entire to you. I had to obey the quiet, deep, wise voice within that was decisive. But that voice (that Child?) had not been heard for so long. It emerged with its own power, yes, but the container was weak, damaged, too threatened by take-over and destruction, adult life echoing those early years. I had to find some reserves of inner strength to push you away, and claim my own space, even if that had to be, for a while, a hospital cubicle under the protections of medical power and concerned builders of that necessary scaffolding. It was enough – just. The squall nearly capsized the boat: I would have drowned. Somewhere there was a will to live, to pull through, those awful months mirroring that lost time of birth, emerging with lungs too full of fluid ...

Considerable action was taken on my behalf by those who

represented the Church in whose border country I min-
istered. There was an unbegrudging willingness to find
some money, and to pay the cost, in terms of time and
emotion, of the added stress of being focal people for the
anxious enquiries of others: to enable therapy and sanctuary, and in crisis to press the levers of power, consulting
with others similarly placed within the institutional structure of medicine. At times it was a question of managing the
unmanageable, of taking responsibility, of using power to
enable some order to emerge from the chaos.

In the midst of this is again that intriguing use of power:
Who knows what? Who can be trusted with information?
Does the reputation of either institution or person need
protecting by the keeping of secrets? These are particularly
sensitive issues for an organization whose concerns range
over the whole of human life, including its intimate details.
The custom of 'public confessions' has never lasted long because it drives people to secrecy and hypocrisy. 'Private
confessions' require respect, despite the fact that they lead
to compromise and, sometimes, others' harm. The problem
is that there is always the danger that the public institution
will invade too much of private life. There are unresolvable
tensions here, not least the constant struggle between openness, honesty, truth and the further honest recognition that
all of us are compromisers at times, none has clean hands,
and the extravagantly pious are usually the ones who have
the least claim to be 'above it all'. None of us is immune to
betrayals and hatreds, jealousies and suspicions, all too often
covered by well meaning intent on the one hand, and collusion in that disastrous assumption that because it is *as
Christians* we are acting, we can do no wrong.

Am I scapegoating when I agree with you that the Church
of England is little interested in its own mental health, let
alone the health of more obvious sufferers, and that we are
living through an ecclesiastical age where only success and

victory are recognised currency, Good Friday but a small cloud that is soon forgotten?

I can point to a fair number of exceptions in the exchanges with me and on my behalf (not least with you!), but I think, in terms of institutional responses by bishops, synods, the press etc, the climate of what is easily talked about and what is shunned, you are right. How often have people come up to me and said, "Thank you for saying what I could never dare say in this church."

I was moved to read of your experience as a Unitarian among Roman Catholic Carmelites. You found them totally devoted to seeking the truth, not claiming to possess it against all others, but living what they had discovered towards communion with all others. It is the fundamental criterion by which churches (and other institutions) can be judged, in both theology and practice: power exercised over against or power shared with?

The television was on and the next programme was *Songs of Praise*. It was the middle Sunday of Wimbledon fortnight and the camera showed a packed crowd surrounding the pristine grass of the new Number One Court, a few weeks before its official opening. Tennis stars past and present contributed their interviews, all in the language of success and triumph, of how faith had helped one to become champion, how songs of victory had echoed round courts and changing rooms, of goals and achievement. The imagery of the hymns matched those of the interviews: the reign of the King was enthusiastically praised.

The assumptions were all about power over others, defeating and winning. We did not hear of power shared, of a game of equally matched players, each calling forth from the other amazing shots that neither had made before, a game that gives the glory to tennis and not to the one who

wins (and what a shame it is that someone has to lose). We
did not hear of the way in which human beings can co-
operate with the divine will and presence, together creating
what is new in the world.

And we heard nothing of the powerlessness at the heart
of faith, of the costliness of love, of power voluntarily given
up for the sake of the other. The empty green rectangle of
a tennis court could not be a symbol of that deeper dimension of human life. And nothing of the kind of king who
does not sit on a throne deigning to notice an occasional
petitioner, but who washes feet and loves whatever it costs:
that kind of love makes you doubt whether 'king' can ever
be a true image of the divine.

So the programme was nothing more than entertainment
by a singalong of cheap religion, a cheerful day out, but not
really different from any other.

Power is so seductive that there is always the danger that
emergency action becomes the norm, that, for example,
power taken by someone democratically elected during a
crisis may not be given back once that crisis is over. Even
the best of regulations are not immune from corruption;
even the most comforting of uniforms may hide the power
to restrict freedom. Of course the person entrusted with
such power has to have the courage to use it wisely where
there is no alternative, but force is to be used minimally and
always to be under the law and held to accountability.
Amputations and the biochemical attacks of 'anti-biotics'
may be necessary to save lives, but we may doubt the wisdom in investing so many resources in awesome, sophisticated 'weaponry' and so little in prevention and education –
gentler methods that take longer and are undramatic. The
parallels between doctors, police, and the military are too
exact for comfort. And do bishops and evangelists act and
preach in a way that is truly that of love?

It was a minor incident, I suppose. I do not often hear an evangelistic appeal from a youth worker to a company of teenagers at a weekend camp. I have been to an occasional rally in my time, and usually felt bombarded. On this occasion I caught a glimpse of what worries me about the enthusiastic evangelical approach.

You began by saying that God had given you a message that morning. (That always disturbs me as a starter: it seems to imply that what you are about to say cannot possibly be challenged.) You held up an egg in front of those teenagers and told them that God wanted to break open their own hard shells and reach the soft and squishy parts inside. You then dramatically smashed the egg, your hand forming as fist as you did so, the yolk and the white spurting everywhere. It was a powerful image, and it will doubtless linger in many minds.

But you portrayed a terrible god, the god of your own unredeemed power. You missed an opportunity. You could have said that God is like a mother hen: God waits, God broods, God gives warmth and protection, God is never a destructive invader. That needs saying again and again because we have all been bruised by those who have had power over us, we have all known our tenderness violated in small or greater measure, we have all built a necessary shell around us for our own protection from further harm. Yes, the shell needs dismantling, may need to be gently tapped from the outside, but at the right time, when we trust we shall be loved in our vulnerable first days of new life. For the chick you destroyed would have emerged in its own good time, with the parent doing nothing. It would have grown towards the moment when it would outgrow the shell, pecking its own way through.

And yet ... There *is* a terrifying aspect of love: the love that is insistent, consistent, that will not let go, that will take you *through* breakdown, breakup, heartbreak, that is with you and in you as you journey. I dare not say that God *caused* my crisis, but I can claim that God keeps faith, keeps contact, keeps loving, bearing with me all the consequences of the misuses of our human freedom.

It felt like being kidnapped. Ordinary folk outside the imprisoning cellar are going about their lives in the colour of a summer day. Inside all is grey, hardly even the contrasts of black and white. You have been snatched suddenly away from everything and everyone that is familiar to you, and you find yourself in a totally alien environment. Others have total power over you, for bane or blessing. There are obvious differences between a hospital and a prison but 'ward' is not too distant from 'warder', and confinement, sometimes solitary, is real enough, kept away from what you desire and from all that is familiar to you. Do those in charge always know from the inside what it is like, so as to be able to be always compassionate? And do the rules allow them? Will their 'inmates' ever see the sun again?

Nowhere do these issues of power impinge on us more poignantly and pointedly than on our lives as sexual beings. The sexual drive is a power indeed and can hold us in its grip, dictating behaviour patterns over which we lose the power of choice. Sexual liberation may look like freedom but may be enslavement. The sexual huntsman may think he is taking risks in the dark, but they are controlled, calculated, almost predictable risks. There is no true abandonment in the joyful mutual giving of love. The rules do not allow it. The vulnerability is but on the surface. We may play into games of control and humiliation: if the other is in charge, we can abdicate responsibility and we can enjoy our lack of worth. And such rituals of coercive power and control can so easily become death-dealing rather than the rituals of creative loving power that are life-enhancing.

Change the perspective a little. Good looks are powerful, they can exercise a 'bewitching' fascination. They give added spice to the drama of hospital soaps. They may evoke more trust than has been earned. A seductive voice may 'captivate'. Add wealth and you have a heady mix indeed. The young especially can exploit and be exploited by it. Inequality of wealth between two people can turn consenting pleasure into dehumanizing mechanics. An attractive law student can make quite a bit on the side to supplement meagre funds, none of which come from an impoverished home. Call it a meal and a bed and a generous gift token: exercising the different kinds of power can give a mutual buzz of excitement. But what of the teenager forced onto the streets night after night whose pimp takes away most of the 'earnings' from a quickie in the back of a car and knocks him about when he does not bring enough money back with him?

Our personal collusions and power traps; the compulsions of habits; the slide from consent and geniality into coercion and cruelty: all examples of another 'power over' us, limiting our freedom and responsibility and holding us back from growing together in love.

Institutional power comes into play too. I was told a story last year. I have no means of knowing whether or not it was true. But it invites long reflection. I start by outlining the facts in as neutral a way as I can.

A clergyman moved from England to a town in another part of the United Kingdom. He founded a community which aimed to serve the goal of reconciliation where there was conflict. He became publicly vocal in criticizing certain local vested interests. Without warning the police came to arrest him at dawn. The charge was child molesting. In jail on remand, while using the lavatory, boiling water was poured over the partition wall from the next cubicle. He was soon released on bail. The case was later dismissed. The charges were not substantiated.

Now I can think of four different scenarios, any one of

which could have been true. As I say, I have no means of knowing. Painfully sensitive issues like child abuse, when they come into the light, either sporadically or, as currently in this country, more systematically, give opportunities to those who seek to reconcile and heal, but also to those who have no scruples about manipulating and causing further harm.

Of course, first, it is possible that this man *had* committed a grave crime, and had harmed a child physically, emotionally, or sexually.

Second though, and more subtly, it is possible that a child, abused by another adult, or an adult with memories and a grudge, out for revenge, placed, or more accurately displaced, an accusation.

Third, he may indeed be innocent of the charge, but the simple fact of a public accusation is enough to ruin his work, and he has to move away.

Fourth, it is possible that a powerful but threatened local group 'arranges' the arrest with the collusion of the police (some of them may themselves belong to that group), thus effectively removing the perceived threat. The police may then publicly apologize for their error.

Accusations, false or true, are powerful weapons in preventing corruption from being brought to the light. Arrest and blackmail, obvious or subtle, the pressure of law and the pressure of what the neighbours will think, these can all come into play against the person who is standing up for an unpopular truth. Institutional power is easily and gravely misused to exclude the troublesome from the common life.

And on the small scale, within families, sex and power are intertwined, however rare obvious and provable abuse may be. Affectionate and erotic touch are near neighbours, and children grow up in a more sexualized atmosphere than we are yet generally able to recognize. Adult sexual feelings towards children may never be expressed in violating

behaviour, but they may well be received as invasive, feed-
ing fantasy and, later, accusations that are false yet carry
with them remnants of truth.

Add to this the climate in which those of my generation
were brought up, when the assumption was that a boy said
a stern No to any incipient sexual desire until he was quali-
fied and able to support a wife. Kisses were always for later
on, a helping hand was an instrument of 'self-abuse', and
the only association of 'wet dreams' was dirt: the sheets had
to be laundered immediately.

The personal events, then, of the last three years, have
alerted me more than ever to the workings and dangers of
power. Maybe one of the unsought gifts from the darkness
is a deeper awareness that leads to an obligation, an inner
requirement, soul-deep, that I warn – for my own protection first, but also for others.

It is a commonplace now to point out that telescopes and
microscopes, computers and video recorders, have vastly
extended our knowledge, taking us to places where ordinary
eyes and ears could not penetrate. For those who operate
the machinery, such power is indeed seductive.

The other side of the world was once far away, and, to
Europeans, unknown not so very long ago. It may still feel
'remote' for me to stay in a scattered rural community in a
sparsely populated corner of Aotearoa/New Zealand, but
the tentacles of the 'worldwide web' easily touch me by
phone and fax and e-mail. The immigration authorities
know I am a temporary visitor, the records of the coach
company will show when I journeyed out of Auckland. The
nearby bush in which it would be easy to get lost feels like
a safe haven from intrusive power which might or might not
operate benignly. (It is also a relief to be given a sense of
proportion by David Hockney's remark that the thing about
hi-tech is that you always end up using scissors.)

Yet my life was saved by an appropriate use of a computer

for a brain scan, and an electric charge from a machine ...

And I was transported safely in murky weather last summer into the docks at Belfast on a brand-new ferry, whose
captain's hand is no longer on the tiller or wheel but a joy-
stick. Nearing land, all he has to do is to keep two dots on
a screen (which come from laser beams in the harbour)
merging into one red dot. When at sea at high speed, if the
electronic communications break down, the ship stops in-
stantly. (Hence the plastic beer glasses.) Power invasive?
Power protective? Power in others' hands for my safety?
Power shared? Trust and abuse?

The morning before that particular sea crossing I had
been to a communion service at the Scottish Episcopal
Church in Stranraer. In most such churches there is a special chair which is usually reserved for the bishop on one of
his occasional visits. A micro hi-fi was sitting on it. I wondered if we were due for an episcopal message broadcast
direct to every church in the diocese, modern technology
reinforcing diocesan unity. But no. The machine played the
part of organ and choir, as backing to help the small congregation sing four hymns from *Ancient and Modern Revised*
('revised', that is, forty-six years ago).

Microphones, loudspeakers, and earphones can of course
be used to help us become more human. The hard of hearing can enjoy public occasions – and also exercise a power
denied the rest of us and switch their hearing aids off. The
radio broadcaster gets used to imagining she is talking to
one or two people in the studio rather than to the thousands
who may be listening – and they too have the power to
switch to another channel. Sensitively placed speakers in a
cathedral enable a congregation to feel they are participating more fully in a service than if a voice echoes from a far
distant altar.

Yet that same technology can exaggerate the megaphone
tendencies of the showman who preaches at you or ha-
rangues you with religious or political dogma. It can produce banks of microphones that turn soloists and groups

into performers rather than leaders and enablers of worship. It can project an event on to a screen in a hall next door, enabling many more people to see what is going on, but distancing them at the same time.

Great art can now be reproduced to high standards on slides and screens, cards and posters. Great music can be appreciated through the recordings of wonderful interpreters. Our eyes and ears can be educated to take time to look and listen, to be contemplative, to pay attention so that something of imagination and spiritual worth is communicated among and between us. Prayer and worship can be enhanced. But the greater the number of people present, the larger the building, the louder the noise, the cleverer the visual sequences, the easier it is for the expert to manipulate and the people to be controlled. Religious leaders, whether in imperial purple or popstar dayglo, have always been falling into the temptations of control through fear or adulation, to be seduced by the illusion that crowds mean success, as though numbers bore a direct relation to truth.

I recall Prospero at the end of *The Tempest*, speaking perhaps for Shakespeare himself, perhaps for all wielders of magic power. He breaks and buries his staff and drowns his book, and places himself in the hands of others:

> Now my charms are all o'erthrown,
> And what strength I have's mine own,
> Which is most faint …
>   … Now I want
> Spirits to enforce, art to enchant;
> And my ending is despair
> Unless I be relieved by prayer,
> Which pierces so, that it assaults
> Mercy itself, and frees all faults.
> As you from crimes would pardoned be,
> Let your indulgence set me free.

❖

So, listening to my guardian angel, or whoever, I need to take this to myself:

I will be careful about talks that I am asked to give, lest they too easily become the well-prepared, well-crafted set piece delivered eloquently from a complete manuscript. Let me refuse the pedestal, the glamour. Let me remember the housebound elderly woman all those years ago in Stretford who said after I had prayed with her, that it had been so beautiful, and that she wished she could pray in words like those I had used. I had not helped her pray better in her own way.

My words can easily oppress and bewitch and not set others free. I may recoil from the preacher with black leather Bible aloft, but I can deliver a mighty verbal punch when I have a mind to. Dangerously, I may not even be aware that that is what I am doing. Using words as magic, to gain control, to have my way, is an abuse.

I have been 'top-heavy' as well. Words come to me easily, 'off the top of your head', not always enspirited and enfleshed from the depths of me, soul-deep, flesh-deep.

So I have had to endure a time of no words. For over a year I was without thinking or reading or writing. I could not sustain a conversation, and very little of what others said could touch me. God was silent too.

Let me take more time to be silent … listen to the body … brood … test the worth of the words. The trees are a kindly but honest audience. Let me prepare myself for a talk more, prepare my manuscript less. Let me remember Laurens van der Post who said he would 'beat about the bush' to startle a phrase into taking wing: he would then follow it, trusting that the words would come.

Let me be as personally vulnerable as I can when I speak, but let me also take care not to be a doormat nor to throw pearls before swine. The less power I exert, the less afraid others will be of me and the more they will trust their story to me. Without dialogue there is no discovery of truth, without story I will never hear other people's truth, and without humour, truth will be distorted by solemnity and self-righteousness. There will be no conversation, no conviviality, no communion.

Debates and arguments, propaganda and ideologies, are the province of those who want to win, and their victory is at the cost of others' defeat. Rarely do those in power willingly and easily give it up. Rarely are they comfortable with silence, and long ago have they given up listening. If I am entrusted with power over others, let me not expect them easily to tell me the truth, and hardly ever to tell me the whole truth. Their health, their homes, their jobs, their families may be in my hands, and they will be afraid.

I knew some of these truths about power before I was ill. Being sectioned three times in five months brought them home. They are part of the furniture now in the house of my being. I cannot escape them, though I may never know them thoroughly enough to become wise.

III
Doldrums

Wandering between two worlds,
One dead, the other powerless to be born ...
Matthew Arnold, *Stanzas from La Grande Chartreuse*

The wind slowly eased and six months after the squall had
hit me, I entered the doldrums. Though still at times anxious and restless, I was for almost a year in a place of nothing happening, nothing doing. My voice was flat. I had next
to no ability to concentrate. I was physically prone much of
the time. I read very little. I can recall re-reading novels by
John Buchan while I was in hospital. Over the next year the
only stories that tempted me were a series of accurately ob-
served and humorous novels by the American writer
Michael Malone; he is a combination of Garrison Keillor,
Alan Bennett, and Charles Dickens. They perhaps occupied
my mind for thirty hours out of, say, eight thousand that
ticked by without meaning. I wrote nothing except notes to
the milkman, and those were strictly professional! I recall
no sexual desire. I was eating reasonably healthily, but without imagination. Survival food at best. Mercifully, I slept
through the night and well into the morning, but I remember no dreams that I may have had.

There seem parallels here with the exhaustion that can
follow overwork, the numbness that follows shock and loss,
an organism that refuses to digest any more *stuff*, and syndromes of chronic fatigue and immune deficiency. Here is a
family of conditions where the biochemistry of the brain
may well be reflecting the state of the body – and the body
politic.

Other pictures and memories float by, from feeling like a
December afternoon at half past three to taking a walk in
the warm gloaming of a June night during what they tell me
was a memorable summer. I could not face the light and
heat and shut myself away indoors. Now that I am awake
and alert again I keep coming across books that were published in 1994 and 1995, annoyed that their publication had
passed me by: most of the time I would expect to see at least
notices and reviews. It shows how the snapshots were few
and how little my camera was used. Most of the days were
blank.

In that dark December of 1994, home at last from hospital but far from well, I would pass slowly round and round
the occasional table in my living room, trying to find relief
from my ever-present restlessness and anxiety. (I was still
taking an anti-psychotic drug.) I would move around for
half an hour or more at a time, now in one direction, now
in the other. I would then gently move myself to and fro in
a rocking chair. Sometimes my eyes would.be shut, sometimes I would look at the holly and the laurel, the laburnum
and the sycamore, the oak and the birch, out there beyond
the window, kind in keeping their distance, neither intruding nor speaking. This I would do for a couple of hours or
more, hoping nobody would interrupt, both wanting
warmth and comfort and unable to receive them, coping
with a visitor, grateful for ten minutes, then wanting to be
on my own. At times it felt like a foretaste of extreme old
age, the rest of the armchairs occupied by others in a similar
state to my own.

It is often foggy in calm weather, making the stationary
traveller turn inwards even more. Most of us dislike fog, especially its thicker and smokier variant, or the cloud that
descends on mountain tops and obscures the view and the
path. But we cannot 'scurry' in fog. (That is a word that
W. H. Auden uses in his poem 'Thank you, fog'.) It is quiet

outside. But it is quite a challenge to find it not boring or frightening, but cosy. Most of the time in my doldrums, I do not think I could have curled up in front of a log fire on a foggy winter day and been even in the slightest degree content ...

❖

You were my most careful visitor during the doldrums. You were not anxious about keeping still and silent and I was glad when you were able simply to sit and to be. You often came at weekends when I was alone in the house, circumstances you thought bleak and empty. I would make you a cup of coffee and you were aware of my slightly stilted movements as I did so. You sat there while I moved around restlessly or rocked myself seeking comfort. I talked to you about the pain of it all, though it was not for a long time that, free at last of drugs, I could begin to *feel* how *awful* those worst times had been.

You saw me living in a kind of limbo, cut off from my inner creative life, finding my inability to write one of the hardest things to endure. I talked of two books that were planned, but I was quite unable to work on them. Though I would listen to music a little, not one book came down off the ever so many shelves. (The Michael Malone novels had come through the post, gifts from a perceptive friend who intuited correctly that my palate might be tempted by them.)

You brought me a painting one day, of the north shore of Iona, the mountains of Mull in the background. It was soothing, and I placed it in the kitchen so that I could look at it while I ate. Sometime later you brought me another, thinking I might like a change. It was of an interior looking out on to a bay and islands: you thought it might stretch my horizons a little. Looking back now, I can think of no reason why I should have preferred either painting to the other, but at the time this second offer threw me. I was easily alarmed by changes, particularly anything unexpected.

You write that you were always glad to see me, even the shadow I had become, and I somehow knew inside that you were a presence I could trust. You were simply there, acknowledging my darkness and lack of hope, clinging on to hope yourself, knowing that many people were holding me in loving thoughtful prayer. Occasionally you would try to find some light in the darkness, suggesting that one day I would be able to use this experience of illness. Now, I think you may well have been right; then, I was scathing and dismissive.

You told me that you reached a point of 'having faith in the waiting', not quite knowing what you were doing, not knowing what was happening in me, perhaps feeling in some measure my helplessness and vulnerability. You were alongside me without fuss, able to be helpless, finding me in pain and finding that painful to endure, yet never once adding to my pain. It was a great gift.

As the months of 1995 went by, you started a new pattern of regularly bringing Sunday lunch to share with me, the menu varied by that Saturday's offering on the Women's Institute homemade goodies stall at Hathersage. Gently heating whatever you brought did not tax me, and you tactfully let me take charge in my own kitchen. As one of my pleasures in life is conversation with friends over a meal, I minded a great deal that I was still staccato: I could not carry a comment or response forward into any kind of flowing exchange. You were aware of how frustrating this was to a hospitable wordsmith. You also saw the irony in that the almost non-existent prayer of that wordsmith had been taken into a fitful wordless groaning.

Every Saturday morning during that year I managed to drive across town for a session of psychotherapy. The process cleared some of the accumulated stress from my double bereavement, not least as it connected with the atmosphere of my childhood. I complained to you early on that nothing much seemed to be happening, and you responded by saying that it had to be like that, since I was in no state for handling deep emotion or for any confrontation. Gradually there was some movement, a loosening, a stretching. One day you asked me to think of a phrase Alan Ecclestone might have used about the pictures and photographs that meant something to him. Almost immediately, I thought of his phrase 'paying attention', valuing what one is looking at until it reveals something of itself. You found this a comfort that the wordsmith's knowledge and skill was not lost, only in storage. I suspect that about this time the anxiety and agitation diminished, but it would be some time yet before I was out of the doldrums. Meanwhile, you continued to listen, a quiet undemanding friendly presence. You were one of that precious company who gave of yourselves to me without asking anything in return. It was part of my healing that the controller had no choice but to receive, and to begin, I hope, to learn to do it gracefully.

Another of the chords that struck home from William Styron's account of his suicidal depression was how he realized he had been most helped by seclusion and time. Seclusion – safety – sanctuary: these are three intertwining words expressing my very deep need in distress. They are in capital letters in an entry in my scrappy diary three weeks after falling ill.

You phoned me to say how upset you were that I had to be in hospital and that you had no 'sanctuary' into which you could welcome me, a safe place with high boundaries around it to protect me from potentially hostile forces ...

Arrangements were made for me to spend a fortnight at a well-known sanctuary, a house of healing in the countryside not far from London. It proved to be a helpful transition from a life focused on the hospital ward to my being able to be at home again. I was enveloped by maternal care, though it took me a week to begin to be able to receive any of it.

And despite being a beautiful and peaceful house, it was set up to handle physical rather than mental illness. Its atmosphere was very upper middle class English – a comfortable country house with chintz. It was also a little too religious for my taste! Not that there was anything overtly pushy, but there was a sense that both it and I would have failed if there had been no tangible blessing by the time I left. One day a delightful young nurse tried very hard to get me to talk, but I was still months away from conversations, and he compensated for his lack of success by turning to prayer, unable simply to sit with me, holding our mutual helplessness in silence.

Nevertheless, there may have been benefit, not least from the opportunities to be 'as I am' in the presence of a counsellor and of two friends, one of whom was on the staff and the other living not far away. You far from abandoned me, even if I found it hard to receive your love. And you, two other friends, who cocooned me in your cars for the frightening journey there and back.

Then I have to make the excruciating admission that a psychiatric ward was for those few months a safer sanctuary than home. Home itself I began to re-arrange. I wanted to retreat to what felt like the safest, most private part – the second attic floor, mainly to a small bedroom with sloping eaves. Symbolically, I moved the books nearest to my heart to another of the rooms there, however unable I was to open any of them.

Apart from the fortnight away, I hardly moved out of Sheffield for nearly a year and a half. I was taken beyond the city boundary only for pub lunches. The villages of High Bradfield and Grindleford on the edge of the Pennines were frontier territory. Beyond lay the land of anxiety. This was yet another irony for the nomad who loved travelling: geographical constriction mirrored the need for the safe and familiar. When I began to drive again, for nearly a year I made two short weekly trips: a mile and a half to Sainsbury's for the shopping and four miles to my psychotherapist.

I remember making an effort to go for short walks.
People would notice me from their windows ... For months
you slouched: there was no spring in your step – you were
bent over, looking much older than your years ... It looked
a brave effort walking the quarter mile to the surgery to
check in every so often with your local doctor. And how
many kindly cars I lowered myself into to be taken elsewhere for a meal: I would shut my eyes some of the time
and ask to be driven slowly, not wanting too much to come
at me too quickly.

The seclusion and time did do their slow work. Gradually
my spine straightened again! But I was of course doing next
to nothing. At some deep level I was saying to the young
child within me, who disliked (and still does) being woken
to a scheduled time by the clock: You can sleep now, resting
for as long as you wish. You will wake up *in your own time*,
your own *good* time, the *right* time.

May Sarton was told when she was recovering from a
stroke that she had no surface energy for the everyday because reserve energy had to be built back first. That feels
like an exact parallel. And nobody knows in advance how
long that will take – except that it will always be longer than
the bewildered controller wants.

❖

It was such a relief in the doldrums when the anxiety and
restlessness eased. It was as if my boat was not moving forward because there was no wind, but was being spun round
and round by some unseen hand below the surface. Then at
last the spinning stopped. I was becalmed, but it felt even
safer to be *still*. I think it was from then on that I began
to reflect again, and to make the kind of connections that
I enjoy and that this book is suggesting. It is of course a
further challenge to carve out more time simply to contem-
plate – a face, a painting, a seascape ... I like Meister

Eckhart's saying that there is nothing in all creation so like
God as stillness.

It was in such a mood that I found myself smiling at a
verse from George Herbert's poem *Affliction* (the first with
that title in the Penguin edition of his poems, the tenth
stanza):

> Now I am here, what thou wilt do with me
> None of my books will show:
> I read, and sigh, and wish I were a tree;
> For sure then I should grow
> To fruit or shade: at least some bird would trust
> Her household to me, and I should be just.

❖

Seclusion is one thing; isolation, its shadow side, quite another. I found myself treading a path between needing help
and resisting the pressure that the simple presence of another person could be. Fellow professionals could be the
worst. Like them, I was used to doing things, and find just
being alongside the most difficult of 'acts'.

'Care in the Community' is thinly spread and I received
no home visits after I had left hospital. Need the lines of
communication have been quite as stretched as they were?
For some months I went along every Friday morning to a
local health centre to collect my ration of pills. Some conversation was offered by one of the nursing staff, but much
of the time I either did not want it or felt unable to take it
up. Certain group activities were on offer, a weekly afternoon of 'Kick-start' excursions, always a surprise. I was
never drawn to participate. A lifetime's dislike of anything
that could be construed as PE, my inability at the time to
cope with anything more than one-to-one sessions, and, I
have to admit, sheer snobbishness about the company, all
conspired to keep me apart. I suspect I am a casualty of
middle-class C. of E., as well as persuading myself to climb
the social ladder, which to my 'aspiring' mother ('upwardly

mobile' but without the necessary wheels) included a religious leg up from my childhood Methodism of the fifties.

So while isolation might have been ghastly, the superficial company of strangers was an even worse prospect. And I felt no desire to get in contact with Depressives Anonymous.

You commented to me one day, "You'll get through this, but you'll do it on your own." And yes, I was totally on my own in that cellar for most of the time, like twenty-three hours a day of solitary confinement, unaware even of the neighbours, who were always tactfully ready to help, but did not intrude.

It was a very simple time, a few ordinary routines, nothing complicated or difficult, with oceans of rest. What conversations there were consisted of little more than 'small talk', but that is not to despise it: making tiny adjustments, learning to accept the long haul. The squall had been so devastating that any talking therapy would have created more turbulence. Indeed, when it began early in 1995, my memories of the first few sessions were of restless pacings and the occasional cry. There were my wordless groans of prayer, and, sometimes, as I switched out the light at night, the simple, Into your hands I commend my spirit.

I took to the vegetables of the *earth*, the root crops of potatoes, parsnips, carrots, swedes, turnips, and to the fruits of *long, slow* ripening – plums, pears, apples, grapes. And meat that had been caught running free – fish, chicken, game. Again, these were simple foods and easy to prepare and cook. I could not cope with the stimulation of coffee, but have always been gently charged by tea. It was a timely gift, that range of tins from Fortnum and Mason!

And three simple statements that I had voiced very early on, which you typed out for me and I kept close by, occasionally reminding myself of them, even if it was only to stare blankly at them.

> There is hope even in my deepest despair.
> I am Jim, and I am bigger than my despair.
> I can and I will overcome it.

❖

If power, whether intrusive, protective, or shared, was the theme I reflected on most as I looked back at the squall, a related but different theme is associated with the doldrums – the powerlessness of being nobody and nothing.

That is what it felt like. Words had gone and the word-smith was reduced to nothing. One of my early fears was that I would be forgotten – within six months no one would remember me, I would be "like a dead man out of mind". I knew that some people could not cope with my being ill: they could not draw near, they withdrew, at best asking a third party from time to time how I was. It was on the record now: I was mentally ill, in psychiatric care, and I had been sectioned under the Mental Health Act.

It had become a second stigma to contend with, along with the one I am all too familiar with, that of being gay. The similarities are painfully acute. To be stigmatized is to be appraised by others not on character and behaviour, but simply on one's membership of a defined category, suspected rather than accepted. Advantage or disadvantage is *in-built*; it pervades the atmosphere of a particular society; the *model* casts its shadow. It is a strategy of distancing: indeed, people often experienced a *physical* reaction, linked sometimes with a feeling of disgust, an uncontrollable reactive movement of drawing back or pushing away. Intellectually, to stigmatize is to declare a category of human beings as no-bodies who are refused access to positions of power, to paid employment, sometimes to housing.

I do not mean by this that I was shunned by everybody; that would be to carry paranoia a stage too far. There is the solidarity of those who have had the same experience as yourself. There are many others who dismiss the stigma as a nonsense and refuse to collude with it. After all, most of those who knew me did not draw back, however much they were touched by a first reaction of not knowing how to respond. But in a similar way to being gay, a mental illness of such seriousness does not help a career structure in most of the organizations in this country which aim to serve *people*.

I am aware that the situation is changing. As there are more exceptions to the old rule, the power of particular stigmas wanes. Also it is true that no one person has to bear all the stigmas of the day, *and* that there can be few people who, however mildly, have not experienced being on the receiving end.

A group of us drew up a series of contrasts one evening under the headings of 'superior' and 'inferior', recognizing that we all knew of occasions when, either for ourselves or for our families and friends, we had been hurt. Here they are:

Boy: Girl.

White: Black.

Master race ruling a quarter of the globe: Colonized people from Welsh to Maori.

English 'a world language': 'no one bothers to learn ours.'

Protestant, 'upright and solid citizens': Roman Catholic, 'breeding like rabbits and wanting to take over the world'.

Christian, 'financially prudent': Jews, 'money lender'.

Educated and fluent: word stumblers with learning difficulties.

Heterosexual and 'normal': homosexual, dirty and disgusting.

Successful career: unemployed layabout.

Sound in mind and body: physically or mentally handicapped.

Married with family: Single, divorced,
    widowed, one parent family, barren.
Smooth-complexioned: blotchy.
Well thatched at fifty: bald.
Washboard stomach: pot-bellied.
Athletic star of the school: inept at ball games,
    the last to be chosen for the team.
Young: Old.
Computerate: not.

"I know it's hard at first to hear what you're saying: it's a bad impediment you cope with. But it only took five minutes to get over my unease."

"Most people don't give me five minutes."

If your stigma is visible, your life is 'constantly precarious': you are discredited, and you have to manage the tensions. So Erving Goffman put it in his book *Stigma*. That is the case for those who are black in a white society. If, on the other hand, your stigma is invisible (such as my two), your life is 'occasionally precarious'; there is always the possibility of being discredited, and you have to manage the information. You calculate, especially in the presence of the powerful, e.g. at interviews for a job. You are aware, with every new meeting, that you carry a secret which you may or may not choose to reveal. You may have 'come out' in the sense that you do not mind who knows, but you are unlikely to be carrying a banner all the time: even the T-shirt needs washing. I may choose to wear a modest badge that doesn't shout a cause or identity at people, that at most invites questions from the inquisitive, and is likely to provoke my cheerful and positive response; but I am unlikely ever to wear a badge that proclaims, "I've been sectioned three times." There is a difference between what feels unjustifiably hidden and what you contentedly hide.

Those who are stigmatized tend to disturb the powers

that be, especially when they discover power among themselves and begin to move towards the table, claiming their place. I like the way Lionel Blue put it somewhere. "Establishments get queasy. The pious get angry. They prefer battery believers to the free range sort."

❖

You kindly gave me permission to tell your story in this book. I have removed identifying detail, partly to protect your privacy, partly to show that its general features are not unique.

You were a young evangelical clergyman, married but troubled by homosexual feelings. At a conference you plucked up courage to tell a brother minister about your problem. He listened to you with respect, you prayed together, and he laid hands on you, asking God that your homosexual desires might vanish. You returned to your room considerably calmer, and later that evening you had what you can only describe as a vision, a strong sense of a personal 'angelic' presence with you. After a while it faded, but the memory, and the reassurance it gave, stayed. But it was not long before your homosexual feelings returned, and over the years you have come to terms quite positively with being gay. Your wife knows, and you are no longer troubled – except occasionally, when you wonder about that experience years ago. Were your evangelical colleagues right after all?

When you told me that story, I asked you to look at it with 'stigma' in mind. Within the society you lived in thirty years ago, and not least in the branch of the Church you belonged to, you took a great risk in speaking out loud of your 'problem'. But you were not betrayed. You had chosen well: your brother minister did not run away, did not denounce you to your bishop, did not urge that you should be unfrocked. He listened, he held your story, and, far from retreating, actually touched you. We may presume that your prayer together was sincere, that God's will be done.

Perhaps the acceptance, the touch, and the prayer provided
the best conditions for that later unusual experience of
the porous boundary between the ordinary and the supra-
ordinary, and you received that reassuring intimation of the
divine. But it still left you with the raw material of your sexuality to work on. It did not remove it, but perhaps it made
the struggle more real, and the material less raw. You had
taken a step away from stigma, away from exclusion and towards inclusion.

The part of you that felt a nobody was coming in from
the cold, and there was less possibility that you would frag-
ment and be reduced to nothing.

Think of another image. Your sexuality, your creativity,
your spirituality sound the same note, but in different oc-
taves. We are familiar with the chords produced by two
people in heterosexual relationships, each contributing his
or her note. Perhaps lesbian and gay people are producing
sounds which are experienced as discordant by so-called
'normal' ears, but that in the melodies of a very varied
humanity, new tunes are being heard, however strange they
may sound at first.

Those of us who are not in a relationship do have to contend with the dangers of 'nothing' as well as the stigma of
'nobody', and I want to draw out some of the implications
of that theme. Whatever our sexual orientation, if we are
more nomads than settlers, and if we are often working with
strangers as part of our job, there is the constant threat of
personal disintegration.

We talk of 'one-night stands', whether a sexual encounter
or the appearance on stage of an entertainer. There are a
number of parallels. In both you are drawing close to
strangers more quickly than may always be prudent. You
have to expose yourself, you are inevitably vulnerable.
There is no other way if there is to be any communication,
let alone any communion. The entertainer has to 'woo' an

audience, be adept at 'warm-ups' or 'fore-play'. The result may be moving, may be full of laughter, may be memorable years after, or it may all go wrong, with a total failure to communicate. You may be hissed off the stage.

It may be worse. The connection I make may be of the 'mesmerising' kind, where, like that politician or evangelist on the 'campaign' trail, I may 'bewitch' you with the magic of wordcraft and 'captivating' eyes. I may dominate you and take away your freedom. Or I might in reverse allow you to do that to me. That would turn genuine communication into 'naked' power and abuse. It is to reduce people to things, indeed to 'no-things'. And we might all love to 'have it' so.

Can the one-night stand be a creative exchange? Undoubtedly yes, but it does indeed have its perilous shadow. If there is no continuity by means of repeat performances, how do you avoid inner disintegration? Or, to put it to those in the helping professions who have constantly to be establishing new relationships, how do you sanctify 'promiscuity'?

In a cohesive society there are inbuilt safeguards: agreed legal frameworks, institutions of marriage and family, a sense of deep belonging to local churches and religious communities. Even the occasional eccentric has a place. There may be an annual reversal of the accepted order to keep the powerful from standing too much on their own dignity, but a feast of fools with a lord of misrule for the day works precisely and only because of the accepted norms of the other three hundred and sixty-four days.

Most of us no longer live in that kind of world. There is much more distance between the 'edge' and the 'centre'. You may well find yourself at a considerable distance from the central support systems, and that very centre itself may be crumbling. Fear and confusion grow at such a time, as does sporadic violence and systemic scapegoating of stigmatized groups.

If you are thus distanced, separated, isolated, if there are

few places in which, or few people with whom, you feel safe
and secure enough to risk being open and vulnerable, if you
collude with others 'pushing away' by fearfully 'drawing
back', if you find yourself 'out of touch' and 'all over the
place', how do you find sufficient resource to prevent, or recover from, collapse, disintegration, despair?

Some of the answers may reveal themselves in the next
chapter. But in relation to feeling nobody and nothing. I
think it is true that you are driven within to explore ways of
healing the splits and divisions in yourself. 'Alone' implies
'loneliness' only when you are aware of being out of touch
with your deeper self, with another, with other people. But
in the aloneness of 'solitude' you create the time and space
to become 'attentive to' and 'engaged with' (to?) that more
profound self (and Self) which some call 'prayer', or with
the raw material of matter, whether ingredients for the cook
or words – genuinely enfleshed and enspirited words – for
the writer; and with the rare gold of a cherished friend. So
you experience at-one-ment and creativity.

   You may also become more 'in touch' as you risk drawing
close to others who are also vulnerable, perhaps more obviously than yourself – those who are handicapped, a young
child, an old man physically dependent in a hospital bed, a
homeless stranger, a refugee in an alien land; any of what
our Jewish ancestors called the 'anawim', the little hardly
noticed people who are especially loved by God, already at
home in the divine domain, the only ones who are so much
already there that they can welcome home the humbled
powerful.

Unexpected gifts sometimes come the way of nobodies and
nothings. If you *know* that a person cannot (or will not)
exercise power over you, love between you can grow true.
Status, class, wealth, and the like, which always cause

divisions, count for nothing: they almost literally vanish, swallowed up by the new dynamic of love.

At the sterner end of such love is the truth that when you have been humiliated, when you are without hope, when you have lost everything, there is no more stripping away to be afraid of. Even death has been swallowed up by love. You can live in constant gratitude. (Thank you, friend no longer with us, for writing that to someone else who also had much to be grateful to you for.)

You moved me when you said that you no longer found me two paces distant, the one who gave the impression of being 'on top of things', who had 'arrived', and on whom you had projected the persona of similar characters from your past. You had enjoyed my sense of humour, quick and rich, but had found it too studied, too self-conscious. Now it was different. I had at least *shown* my vulnerability, and love could flow. Now you find you can talk to me about any-thing because you know I've been there. There is a new note of compassion because I did not entirely flinch from the desolation and try to seal it off. (Actually I did try but it didn't work!) For you to know that there are large tracts of my life where I have no control, where I am unable to *do* anything, where I am as helpless as the next person, of which I even have no memory: that has triggered your trust. And what greater gift could you give me?

There is a parable that reflects that. Scrawled on an arch of a bridge over the river at Portadown in Northern Ireland, among the hard-edged political slogans of "Brits out" and "Orange and proud" is the vulnerable humanity, age-old, ever fresh, of "Anthony loves Elaine", the 'loves' symbol-ized by the well-nigh universal heart with an arrow through it. At least the possibility is still alive that the little people will one day inherit even that troubled part of the earth.

There is another parable in the story of James Baxter, one of this century's best Pakeha poets in Aotearoa/New

Zealand. He founded a community with and among the Maori peoples in the middle reaches of the Wanganui River in the North Island. The community was a haven for the destitute.

He wrote a journal while he was there, later published as *Jerusalem Diary*. He became aware that the poor are blessed not because they are good but because they are empty. It's the same theme – becoming nothing, the void on which Te Wairua Tapu (Maori for 'Holy Spirit') moved at the beginning of the world, and still moves. Each of us is a mass of faults and contradictions, but it is only when we forget that we are not good that our lives backfire on us.

He went on to write of the mental poverty that the writer must one day face. He felt himself to be like a corpse that "swells up and gives off a stink of words". Like him I suppose I do it "for money and kudos". When words become mental possessions, perhaps we can write if we then forget what is written and insert a health warning: It will damage you if you swallow any of these words whole. (I rather like the story, I think by Primo Levi, of the wordsweeper in the sky who brushes away every night all the words that have risen up that day, the 'hot air' from the surface of the earth.) If words can become dead leaves, they "do not clog a stream for ever. The smoke of rubbish can be shifted by the wind."

James Baxter tells us that the Maori distinguish three kinds of poverty: 'nga pohora', the poor; 'nga mokai', the fatherless; and 'nga raukore', the trees which have had their leaves and branches stripped away.

I can recognize them now as my brothers and sisters in that extended family of the divine domain (called by some the Kingdom of God). I am not always yet at ease with them, but woe is me if I pass them by with my nose in the air. James Baxter's critics urged him to expel the troublesome from the community, not least the habitual vagrants drifting in and out of prison in a haze of alcohol. "But I will never take their advice. If 'nga raukore' were pushed out, the blessing of God would go away with them, and the foundation of the community would be blocked up with stones."

✤

Another gift from 'down under' these past eighteen months of slow recovery was some words of Peter Newall in an article called 'On being refined' in the Australian magazine *Eremos*. He had been intrigued by a reference that the American writer Annie Dillard had made to some Arctic explorers, whose frozen corpses had later been recovered. In their pockets had been found some silver cutlery, dinner place settings engraved with personal initials and family crests. That vivid picture causes Peter Newall to reflect thus. I find it a statement that sums up so much of what was happening during my months in the doldrums, most of the time unbeknown to me, now beginning to take some shape. I'm even humbled by not being able to think of a better way of expressing it. So I quote:

"Pilgrims of the inner journey sense a magic in themselves of being new and strange and better. The function of that feeling is to give the courage to stand alone. For to be at ease from yourself is to be delivered also from theological, ideological foes and friendly collectives alike. There is much less sensation in life, less passion. Nor is there any more exultation in 'spiritual' triumphs, no heartburn in defeat, no smarting hours after the event. That 'every valley is exalted, every mountain and hill made low' in our inscape signifies that the highest ambition now open to us is to become an ordinary pilgrim, shorn of distinctive badges and without authority. Yet early on it is painful to forego the initialled silver place settings and the uniforms of fine true blue. But when we ask for God to walk with us, this is but the fringe of an imagined glory we are letting go. Aloneness is to be singular without effort – it is like loneliness but without the smudged passion and defeat. It is a stable ordinariness, plain, uncoloured, and for some it is accompanied by a felt independence of much that gave life the

colour we loved: music, art, writing. We did not expect God
to move us on from such pleasures, though we are aware
that we own an image of some 'leaving all and following
him'. Was it heroism in them? It isn't with us, more like
having lost or misplaced an appetite. There is an appetite
for security, for balm, for uninterrupted vision. We own it
when it is gone, when we sink in waves of grief and, struggling to hear his answering word, find it strange. 'Expect
nothing.' he says, 'Wait.' And so there come long seasons
when the promised precincts of new heaven, new earth, new
life give place to the tiny courtyards of today where, if I am
to hear his voice, I am not to harden my heart against the
limits made for me."

So it is that I have wanted to listen not to symphonies and
concertos: the orchestras will not fit in the tiny courtyard.
But a handful of chamber musicians will. It is, in a way,
more demanding music, for it challenges me not to flinch
from the fire of intimacy.

Sonnets and haiku appeal more than epics, and I detect a
shift in what I find myself writing: details of a travel diary,
one or two short stories, an occasional short poem. (None
for publication ... well, not yet.)

It is also the case of less religion and more life – not per-
fect life for fragile minds and bodies, that is not possible,
but a quality of life, glimpses of the 'eternal' at the heart of
particular events here and now.

I want to return more directly to the notion of stigma and
the experiences of being nobody and nothing. It was a case
of the right book at the right time, though I nearly passed it
by because of the title, *Jesus : A Revolutionary Biography*. It is
by John Dominic Crossan, an Irish-American Roman
Catholic New Testament scholar of some repute. When it
came into my hands I was feeling strong enough to tackle

this version of a more academic work, written for a wider readership. (My concentration span still does not feel quite up to *The Historical Jesus*, but that now may be a lazy excuse.) I connected with him because he argued that the truly revolutionary aspect of what Jesus said and did was that he crossed the taboo boundaries of his Jewish culture to touch, by word and deed, the untouchables, the nobodies of his day. He did this not to begin a new religion, but to *incarnate* and *communicate* this quality of life which is eternal and indestructible, a life of risky and vulnerable love. His touch, whether of a woman who was 'unclean' because of an unstoppable flow of blood, or of a suspected foreigner with an equally 'impure' skin disease, demonstrated that the stigmatized person was *already* a citizen of the Commonwealth of God, independent of character and reputation. The outcasts from societies built on principles of division, including religious ones, by the very fact of their excluded status, are given free entry tickets into the divine domain. Of course you have the freedom to tear the ticket up, but all I have to do at those old pearly gates is to read what it says on my two tickets, 'Gay', 'Sectioned'. A friend, with typical exaggeration (perhaps it is no coincidence that he is Irish-American too!) pushed the point home, telling me that I had done too much giving for my own good, and that he hoped I would spend the rest of my days enjoying simply receiving. Well, I still have to earn a crust, which probably is a lack of trust, but I'm open to any proposals for enjoyment!

Jesus touched the stigmatized in an act of healing which went deeper than a cure. In itself a cure merely postpones death for a few years. Rather is it true that to be welcomed and included, to be never let go of, *is* to be healed. Jesus further enacted this message by eating with them too, which again broke taboos. (Also welcome were the powerful who made themselves vulnerable to criticism because of great need – a Roman centurion and a tax collector, the one a soldier of, the other colluding with, the colonial occupying power.)

Dominic Crossan renders the beatitude, "How blessed are the poor" as "Only the destitute are innocent." He sees in that the key to the manner of a person's release from the trap in which he or she is held. Why is it that only the destitute are innocent? It is because, utterly deprived, they have no power to inflict injury on another. They are free from blame. They have been totally sinned against. They are dependent on others for every gift, every grace. For them, a crumb *is* salvation.

Whether any one person is in fact so completely destitute is a moot point. But there is this tract of territory, inner and outer, for each and all of us, that *is* destitute. When we are inhabiting or traversing that territory, often a stigma, we need someone, the grace-giver, with the gift of silence and non-intrusive presence. A non-possessive touch and a tactful crumb may help. But a signal will have been given that the destitute one, perhaps our silenced and forgotten inner child, has found a trustworthy listener who will pay profound attention to our unique profound story, to its point of greatest pain and abandonment. It may be a story that we ourselves hear for the first time in the telling, one which we can barely articulate, one which we will communicate at best in fragments of language. But in the very telling in the presence of welcome and respect, we hear the spring of the trap released: we *know* that we are of *infinite* worth, that we all belong together in our humanity in God.

Therefore, trust no evangelist who is not completely at ease in the territory of your pain, who fears for his reputation if he is stigmatized along with you, who cannot be still and silent and *wait* for *you*, through *your* story, to reveal the Gospel to *him*. The one who comes with gifts most confidently has yet to hear his own yearning, for the other as Christ-for-us wanting to recognize and greet the Christ-in-us, however long may be the wait for that 'saving encounter'.

That kind of touch, that kind of welcome, gives a momentary experience of a different way of life from that in

which we live most of the time: a death-defying, life-
enhancing, love-making communion and community. No
wonder it provoked the powers that be to opposition. No
wonder that the powers that be can never, at least while in
role, hear good news of liberation. And perhaps no wonder
that such a new life was understood as resurrection life as
well as eternal life, visions and appearances after Jesus's
death affirming and deepening the convictions first sown in
those sporadic encounters during his life.

For me, it was a new conversion, a penny-dropping
moment of disclosure, a historian's considered opinion about
what was at the heart of Jesus's mission meeting a profound
personal need at a moment when I could receive it. I am
tempted to write about Dominic Crossan's work at length,
but it would be an inadequate if enthusiastic précis. Better to
recommend to anyone feeling pushed out: read chapter
three: its title is 'A Kingdom of Nuisances and Nobodies.'

I have one further reflection. Dominic Crossan has been
taken to task by the Vatican, and his most substantial schol-
arly critics are the Roman Catholic Raymond Brown and
the evangelical Anglican Tom Wright. It may be unfair to
say that their work is to interpret Jesus in a more overtly religious framework, but I think they are more acceptable
than Dominic Crossan to religious establishments, and
themselves nearer their centre. But I wonder whether it is a
coincidence or not. Life in all its fulness or dogma in all its
correctness? I know that 'dogma' and 'doxa', 'teaching' and
'praise' are closely linked but how can that connection come
alive in an age which is no longer automatically accepting of
religious institutions, but is deeply concerned about the
quality of life? Are some scholars beginning to help us give
shape to Bonhoeffer's, 'religionless Christianity', a phrase of
prophecy from more than fifty years ago?

These reflections led me to consider how any exercise of authority that is consistent with the way of Jesus needs to be

built on the experience of being nobody and nothing. For most of its life the Christian Church has had three 'orders of ministry', deacon, presbyter, and bishop. Each order has its dilemmas about the use of the power that comes with the authority of an 'office'. There are parallels in other organizations. The question for all those in positions of leadership are similar: How is authority and power to be exercised?

The deacon's order of ministry takes the servant as its central image. In practice in the early days of the Church the deacon had considerable power, often acting as an ambassador for a bishop. How is such power to be exercised as a *service*? The word, however, obscures the radical shock at the heart of Jesus's 'servant' action of washing the disciples' feet. He took on the role of a *slave woman*, whose duty was to welcome guests whose feet would not have been all that sweet smelling after a journey along hot and dusty roads. But as the Church increased in influence and then in power, the originating symbol seems to have been forgotten. If we were to give due weight to the scandal of putting nobodies at the centre we would have reason to expect that the disclosure of a stigma would rank high on the list of qualifications for ordained ministry.

The presbyter's order of ministry goes further. Its central image of the priest is that of sacrifice, of the whole burnt offering, of holocaust. It implies the putting to death, the annihilation of the ego, surface, grasping, greedy, possessive, status-seeking self. That is what is involved in becoming truly priestly.

Only with those experiences branded into one's whole being can a person be trusted with oversight and its necessary powers. The purpose of the use of such authority is the enabling of other people's and the community's flourishing. It is to be exercised with and among and not over or against. Action is preceded by listening, is coercive only in extremis, and even then seeks a deeper Yes beneath the necessary No. That is the ministry of the bishop, of the one whose eye is to be on the whole, so as to encourage the right decisions for the good of the whole. It is not all that different from the role of the charge nurse or hospital chief administrator, of social services director or managing director. If the Christian task is distinctive, it is only by pointing, by word and deed, to the deepest implications and cost.

For these ways of being and doing are at their best if they are pioneering a truly *human* being, doing, and living. If it implies the stigmata of branding, it is to share in our common human woundedness, to recognize that our own stigmas are welcomed, and to know that the only power that nobodies can trust is that of a love prepared to be emptied to the point of apparent total nothing, embracing a dying that a fuller life be born.

IV

Zephyrs

STRETCHING   I had been becalmed – or my boat had been in dry dock. By the autumn of 1995 it was ready to be tested in the quiet waters of the harbour. Or the faintest of breezes stirred the millpond. I was beginning to move again. I pottered around in the sunshine, ever so carefully stretching and looking about me and taking an interest again in the wider world.

You had seen me in the spring of that year, noticing that some energy was returning. You saw a plant that had been dying beginning to recover: water was flowing up from the roots, bringing green back to withered leaves.

SMILING   I wonder when it was that I first smiled again, my inner child able to chuckle. I do remember queuing at the check-out at Sainsbury's a week or so before Christmas that year. The muzak included a sugary rendering of *Mary's Boy Child*. We were reminded of the angels and bidden to "listen to what they say", when the music was interrupted by, "Tracy Lee to Central Cash please, Tracy Lee to Central Cash" – "because of Christmas Day." Then we were treated to *Adeste fideles*, the only time Latin had been heard that year in the supermarket. The management was probably softening up the customers to buy togas in the post-Christmas sales.

LISTENING   My attention span began to increase. By the autumn I was able to go with you to a few chamber music concerts hosted by the Lindsay String Quartet at the Crucible Theatre. It felt daunting at first – you surmised correctly. I was nervous. Who I would bump into? What would usually be a pleasant surprise when I am well might easily have been a numbing shock as I took my first tentative steps back into the public world. The music was kinder, and I have been increasingly able to let Haydn, Beethoven, and Schubert contribute to my healing: oddly enough, not Mozart. It is a superficial dismissal of his music to say he was too cheerful and was not able to meet me in the depth, or at least in my depths. But that is how it felt.

❖

GROUNDING   I have already noted that your advice to eat vegetables that had grown in the ground suited my palate and the overall state of my organism. I have become ever more fond of the rooted potato slowly baked!

This reflects one of my life questions which came to a focus in my illness. I had certainly become 'ungrounded', some of the time 'on a high', in a world of fantasy. I discovered that I was still too much on my mother's ground: my own rootedness was compromised. Where do I stand? Add to this a nomadic temperament, an ability to be temporarily at home in many places but never putting down roots, never a neighbourhood or local person, not your regular vicar, and acute danger was never far away. Years ago I remember warming to a remark of the folk singer Pete Seeger, that his roots were not in places, but in people he could laugh with, sing with, grieve with. The trouble is that we need somewhere to lay our heads if we are not totally rooted in God. (And who ever was, except One?) We need protectors when the weather turns bleak and cold, and a hurricane looms. And those familiar with the energy patterns of the body speak of the root chakra at the base of the spine, storehouse of memories of our personal and corporate past. Few of us can visit that place and find it untroubled.

I like the word that Eckhart uses: 'grunde'. It can mean 'ground', also 'inner core' or 'kernel', perhaps 'seedbed', which gives the sense both of earth and of potential for growth, of the seed which has to die, of being 'rooted and grounded' in the incarnate God whose name is Love.

TOUCHING   Grounding is a near neighbour to touching. Am I 'in touch', with genuine 'con-tact'? For loss of touch was one of the keys to my crisis. At a fundamental level I was mourning a touch I had never had and now never would, a quality that, for all the warmth and affection, was compromised in infant days, and a quantity that was miserly, leading to a deep sense of deprivation. It was a loss that I had known *about* for years, had in some degree explored, but I knew it again, more critically, when I saw life ebbing from my mother's now shrivelling flesh-body, in intimate touch with whom I had been born. Only then is the loss final, and absurd hope has at last to die.

That reality gives another dimension to the way Dominic Crossan interprets 'Gospel' as coming home to people: when the untouchable is *touched*. The adult who has been distortingly touched in infancy, who is therefore wary of touch, and feels unworthy of touch, may be surprised to a moment of healing by a touch which is routine to the other. I can remember being enveloped by a Maori woman who held me close in welcoming embrace, my head disappearing between her breasts; it was a mother's touch of unconditional love.

Different skin textures are mixed up with this, some of which nourish us, some of which alienate us. And those textures can change over the years, disturbing us when what was a point of contact becomes tact-less.

Touch can be more profoundly memorable than words, though the two together, the one giving even greater depth to the other, can make a moment resonate through the years. Touch can humiliate and 'dis-grace' or it can show what no other gesture can. It can be 'grace-ful' and show the 'body's grace'.

I can *see* for miles across the Hebridean seas as I write, a yacht skimming towards Lewis. I can *hear* only for yards, as a child playing in the garden below me laughs with delight. But I can *touch and be touched* only when another person approaches me, feet and then inches away, distance eliminated.

You came with a different touch, that of the healing masseur, working down through layer after layer of knots in the muscles of my back, neck, shoulders, legs, and feet. You also channelled healing energy, simply being present and letting go of any expectations of how I should be or what you should be doing. But that on its own would have been immensely frustrating. The touch mattered, the touch stirred the matter, moved the energy that was stuck, preventing it from turning in on itself once more. But that touch was clear and not intrusive. You did not cut into and damage the chrysalis. You let the darkness be in which transformation takes place, and from which the butterfly emerges unharmed.

The revived custom of exchanging a gesture of peace at the communion service has caused great confusion and controversy precisely because we do not know what kind of touch is appropriate. Very few literally express the 'Kiss of Peace', while others shy away from a handshake. This is a particular instance of a more general discomfort: bodies that are at ease with touch have not been taught to be so by anything they have heard and seen in churches. A book of prayers and a packet of condoms do not sit easily together by the bedside lamp.

There are moments, of course, when it is different, when the desire to love and be loved overcomes fear, and each

opens something of heart and flesh to the other. It is a touch
that affirms, heals, and stirs, all at the same time. When we
relax into the pleasure of it, even tummies rumble in appre-
ciative delight. Of course we want such moments to be
more than occasional 'happy accidents', we want continuity
to contain mutual desire, repeated and varied touch yielding
ever more fruit.

My own experience of creativity in solitude, touching
words, relishing them, playing with them, creating something new with them, is profoundly *sexual/spiritual*. It would
be pious claptrap to go on to say that such *spiritual/sexual*
satisfaction comes at the cost of a refusal to enjoy the other
gifts of touch that are on offer. So often we simply do
not recognize that the protections we have built around
ourselves from fear of further harm are now unnecessary
defences. We can dismantle them to embrace, however
vulnerable we feel, a more richly embodied loving. In its
turn that love will feed the creativity of solitude, lending it
more ease and less pain.

That is not to deny the joy of the 'happy accidents', keeping
hope alive, putting a spring in your step. Such gifts of touch
are not those that come from continuity, but from William
Blake's kissing "a joy as it flies". It is the brush of the fawn's
flesh as it stops momentarily in the forest glade, lithe and
liquid, nostrils quivering in the sun. Then with one bound it
is away. To try to tether the fawn is life- and love-denying.
The encounter can be joyful only with a light touch.

Your touch that day, stranger that you were to the contexts
of my life, was firm, dry, comfortable, connected. It was
clear, open, friendly, imposing no agenda. It was alert to
possibility, empty of direct sexual intent, yet full of sexual
potential. It was life-enhancing, love-hinting …

WALKING The grounding that has been part of my recovery has heightened the vertical movements of walking as
well as widening the horizontal movements of touching!

Even when I was in hospital, there were not many days
when I did not walk at all. It may have been a slow slouch at
worst, a heavy pacing of the corridor in a vain attempt to
find a rhythmic comfort. But I remember working out a fif-
teen minute round of the hospital grounds – mostly on my
own but sometimes in company. (You commented that you
trotted while I walked; there must have been some energy
available to me.)

Walking has always been my favourite outdoor pleasure
(well, almost ... and certainly the most frequent and regular), and my only reasonably continuous form of exercise.
Ideas, thoughts, connections come to me as I walk, and
many are the addresses I have first tried out on the trees.
The Latin tag 'Solvitur ambulando', 'It is solved by walking', was never far from my awareness in those worst of
times. Certainly, in the doldrums, not many days were without a walk of at least half an hour round local park and
wood. I am so thankful I did not have to tramp and pace the
city streets.

It is significant that my first independent trip from
Sheffield, in the October of 1995, was to Malvern, for not
only was there a safe house with friends there, but those
modest hills for a couple of short walks in the autumn sunshine and the clean air. Later on I returned to the mode of
walking which has an end in view, though with time built in
for diversions and the unexpected and a shorter distance
than once I would have planned. For now, a meandering
circle was fine, and no need to consult a watch. My ikon was
Wainwright's boot: a camera filmed the redoubtable fell
walker of the Lake District in his old age – he had always
advocated watching where you are putting your feet and
treading with a firm gentleness that would compact the path
and not erode it. Grounding and walking, solidly together.

I scribbled a quotation on a hospital appointment card

when I was ill and I cannot remember its source. The style makes me fairly sure it is no longer in copyright!

> Above all, do not lose your desire to walk. Every day I walk myself into a state of well-being and walk away from every illness. I have walked myself into my best thoughts, and know of no thought so burdensome that I cannot walk it away ... [T]he more one sits still the closer one comes to feeling ill. Thus if one just keeps on walking, everything will be all right ...

There is a nice gloss on this in May Sarton's remark that she was better able to cope with tension at seventy than she had been at fifty because she had learned not to force herself but to *glide*.

CYCLING   Ideally, if not always in practice, I am drawn to walking first and using a car last, with cycling, public transport, and taxis coming between in my order of priorities. So in the summer of 1996 I found that energy and enthusiasm had sufficiently returned to participate in a trail-blazing ride from Belfast to Land's End. It was organised by the engineering charity Sustrans (ie *Sus*tainable *Trans*port) as part of its efforts to establish a national cycle network of 2500 miles by the year 2000 and 6000 miles by 2005. We had to make our own arrangements for accommodation, but during the day the only thing we had to do was pedal (and push), luggage being taken for us in vans, marshals posted at every doubtful junction, and refreshments supplied by various communities en route. You could enjoy the view of the lycra shorts ahead, or conversation with a companion at your side, or drop back for a while on your own to muse and admire the wider view. I wrote about it afterwards as the ride of the little people, the theme of nobodies still in mind, and wondered about an international millennium tax to fund a bicycle for every person in the world, provided they passed a test for road sense and simple maintenance. But the highlight personally was two minutes of exhilaration as I swept off Exmoor with sun, wind, and rain together on my face. I knew I was alive again.

I am not well read in Friedrich Nietzsche, but I came across this quotation, and it fits exactly with what I felt that August afternoon:

> Gratitude pours forth continually, as if the unexpected had just happened – the gratitude of a convalescent – for convalescence was unexpected ... One is all at once attacked by hope ... the intoxication of convalescence after long privation and powerlessness: the rejoicing of a strength that is returning, of a reawakened faith in a tomorrow and the day after tomorrow, of a sudden sense and anticipation of a future, of impending adventures, of seas that are open again, of goals that are permitted again, believed again.

NAMING   It is an old belief that to name someone or something is to have control over that person or thing, or at least to understand a little better, perhaps to be able to come to terms with whoever or whatever. But it felt double-edged to receive the diagnosis of 'severe reactive depression'. It was a comfort to know that others had been this way before, that I was not under the influence of an unidentified virus, that I could be reassured that with time I would get better, and that there was no reason why, with care, there should be any recurrence. But a general label did not meet the uniqueness of the person who was undergoing this trial and tribulation. I did not remotely feel in control, though I did learn a little about the syndrome, and I did begin to come to terms with the agenda it set me: seclusion, time, rest, medication, therapies of talk and of touch. What it has also done has been to turn the question inwards. Who am I? What is my name, my true character?

That exploration has taken me along some fascinating byways. Whoever wrote out my medical record on the ward had given me 'John' as my first name before crossing it out and substituting the correct one. Now that was odd. I don't know if other Jims are ever addressed as John, but it happens to me quite often, and it doesn't always seem a slip of the tongue. An obvious explanation is that both names begin with the letter 'J' and end with a nasal consonant, 'n' or 'm'. But the varied contexts in which the mistake has been made have caused me to speculate in territory where I am a sceptic.

A woman who used to come to me regularly for counselling some years ago, whose hold on the everyday was insecure, but whose intuition could be sharp and clear, often addressed me as 'John'. I remember a dream in which the figure of a man appeared whom I recognized as an 'angelic' carer, and his name was the Greek John 'Johannes'. According to one of my friends John is a heart name, and that accords with the sense I have of needing to draw on the energies of feeling to which I do not have easy access. Perhaps I project the name John on to them. I have always been drawn to the figure of the Beloved Disciple in the Fourth Gospel, the one who was physically and emotionally close to Jesus. Some have argued that his name was John, like the apostle to whom the Gospel was attributed (or dedicated).

So on a number of counts I am drawn to the name. There is also a weird story. Some years ago I was taking a meditative walk on an early summer morning around Brompton Cemetery in London. My attention was not being drawn towards a tourist interest in gravestones and epitaphs, but for no apparent reason I found myself stopping by the grave of John Snow. I later recalled that he had been a doctor in nineteenth century Soho, the discoverer of the waterborne character of cholera and one of the first people to experiment with anaesthetics. His work led to significant improvements in the water supply and consequently in the public health, and the use of anaesthetics considerably reduced the amount of pain suffered through surgery. Not many doctors can claim so to have improved the human lot. On his gravestone were the exact dates of his birth and death, and I felt a shiver down my spine when I calculated that when he died he had been to the day the age I was that morning. A passing dog-walker to whom I enthused about this amazing news muttered that such coincidences are statistically inevitable once in a while. The sceptic in me grinned, but I went back for breakfast also muttering – about reincarnation – and his name was John ...

Or could it be true that there are beings who guide us and protect us, whose names we may or may not know? A friend is convinced that we have 'spirit guides' who come and go, who make soul-deep connections with us at times of crisis. Another friend was convinced that my current guide is an ancient Chinese man with a sense of humour. And guardian angels? Again I can witness only to another's conviction that each of us has a stable, protective, guiding presence throughout our lives, who knows whence we have come and the work we are called to fulfil in this particular lifespan.

I do know that a dream gave me 'Christopheros', 'Christ Bearer', as the name of an angelic presence. I scribbled a note a few days before I was ill that it felt that, to quote the hymn, angels in bright raiment had rolled a stone away. If they had, the trouble was that too much life was released and I was unable to earth and contain it. And that may well be true ...

Intuition also wrote with intensity that angels with hovering wings were protecting both myself and somebody close to me, through a storm that had already broken. More quietly, though I do not exactly know the truth I am writing, I believe they were protecting me through the squall. Whoever you are, whatever your name and nature, previous incarnation, spirit guide, guardian angel, John, Christopheros, I greet you. Guard me. Guide me. Your names are part of me.

As are the genes of my ancestors – dark cruel grandfather,
rigid cool grandmother, gruff upright grandfather, warm
long-suffering grandmother, each of you vague in my memory since you all died when I was a child; more clearly and
obviously, my mother and father, your passions for God and
man entangled, yourselves children and parents of your
time, affectionate yet anxious, shining brightly as the sun
yet by that very brightness casting a shadow and hiding
darkness, steadfast and cheerful; more tantalizingly, great
grandparents, the Cotters, then of Dublin but a generation
before that of County Cork (where an aristocratic family
history has more than its fair share of Jameses and Church
of Ireland clergy); the Macarfraes of Ireland and Scotland
(the father of one of whom having been Captain Grimenga,
a Dutchman, master of a tea clipper, buried in Bombay –
and another was clerk to the Curragh, the racecourse in
Dublin); the Barringtons, farmers originally around
Bowdon in Cheshire; and the Englands of Lancashire,
north of Manchester. I can hear the teasing of my friends at
some of those connections!

James was inevitable for my first name, for it was my
father's too, and both grandfathers'. The best laid parental
plan was to address me as Jimmy as a child but James later
on (to avoid confusion with my father who was known to
everyone as Jim). But I refused, finding James too formal for
anything but my signature and legal documents.

Owing to a feud on my mother's side of the family, I was
given the second name of England to placate certain rela-
tives of my grandmother. Had I been called after my maternal grandfather I would have been named James
Barrington Cotter, which might have done much for my career but might well not have been for the good of my soul.
It does have a certain ring to it even so …

As it was, 'England' caused me enough trouble, from the
mockery of schoolmates to the disbelief of an Italian police-
man looking at my passport after a students' holiday
mishap. I am still not sure how kindly my Latin teacher was

being when he gave me this verse:

> His second name is England,
> And his first name it is James,
> Now that's very right and proper,
> For they're both good British names.
> But his last name is not proper,
> An improper name is Cotter,
> For Cotta was a Roman.
> And Cotta was a rotter.

Still, I soon learned to cheer myself up with this:

> There'll always be an England,
> And England shall be free,
> If England means as much to you,
> As England means to me.

All that is a little trivial, but successive 'namings' have been important, and I honour the name of my ancestors, and I try to appreciate the material they have passed on to me, even their unfinished agendas, everything unresolved in their own lives to which they were not able to give a name.

I have glossed over 'Jimmy', not because he is insignificant to the adult Jim, but because my therapy included a good deal of work on his story, and most of it is private. Suffice to say that the tale includes devouring monsters with ravening appetites that could never be satisfied (some of *their* names are Eros, Libra, and Labor), whose truest names, unrecognized, were protectors of the treasure that was the wounded infant Jimmy, and indeed of that frustrated raging baby himself. If they have not yet been completely reconciled, they have at least been introduced.

I half knew these things twenty years ago. They need our caring attention for longer than we think. But again I remember encountering Auden's poem 'For the Time Being', in which the Star of the Nativity summons the three wise men and challenges them to say "I will" to "tortured Horror roaring for a bride":

>Then wake, a child in the rose garden, pressed
>Happy and sobbing to your lover's breast.

In another phrase, he tells of the child "who speaks of long ago in the language of wounds".

At one moment a couple of years ago that young Jimmy was not so much speaking or roaring as growling, a good rumbling word from a not quite yet pacified trio of monster, baby, and adult caring Jim. The naming may have been accurate in the past, but my intuition, imagination, mind recognized a truth long before beginning to embody it and touch its heart.

Two pictures delight me and encourage me. They have become for me images of a contented Jimmy at Christmas. One is a card sent to me in 1979, a photograph of a Mother and Child, a sculpture in stone (with no indication of either place or sculptor). The infant Jesus is sitting on his mother's lap; she is smiling, and he is *chuckling*. It is an unusual depiction for both art and theology, a delight nevertheless. And I also remember years back conjuring with the name 'Laughing Water': certainly the chuckle of a mountain stream on a summer afternoon is a healing sound.

The second image is from Leboyer's book on childbirth, *Birth without Violence*. It is a photograph of a baby soon after birth, eyes closed, with a facial expression as serene as a Buddha. Matching it is another such photograph, the baby's eyes open in wonder.

What interests me now is that I came across these pictures years ago, but they struck me enough to keep them. It is as if I noticed them then but have recognized them now. There has been an encounter with the inner Christ-ened infant. He is now part of my name. The baby has come closer to my heart.

From some reclaiming of the past to an unknown future: the Scriptures point to a promise that we shall be given a new name, known only to the one who receives it, (Revelation 2.17) written on a white stone, that symbol of integration. The thought is comforting, and it leads me to my favourite story from the Jewish Scriptures, that of Jacob wrestling with a stranger (Genesis 32.22–32).

'James' is the English translation of the Hebrew 'Jacob'. I am not immediately pleased, since it means 'Deceiver' or 'Cheat', the one who hoodwinked his father Isaac into depriving his brother Esau of his birthright. Another translation is 'Heel Clutcher', the second twin who, as he was being born, was holding on to his brother's heel.

Jacob fled from his home, cheating and lying his way through the years as he worked for his uncle Laban, acquiring two wives and considerable wealth in the process. Then he turned for home and on reaching the river Jabbok cowardly sent his whole company on before him to act as a buffer against Esau whom he knew he had to encounter the following day. He was left alone by the ford, where (in a dream?) he wrestled the night through with a stranger (angelic?). Jacob was wounded in the struggle but would not let go of his protagonist. He inquired his name, but was challenged to give his own. It was the moment of truth; he admitted, with his name, all that the name had implied. The stranger would not give his own name, thereby revealing himself to be a messenger for the unnameable God, but he blessed the truth-aware Jacob, and gave him a new name, Israel, "because you have striven with God and prevailed."

To what degree these last years of struggle could be called a struggle with God I do not know. But they have certainly involved some difficult truth-delving and I am at ease with being known, as one of my 'names', 'Godstriver', along with the 'Wordsmith' already claimed. I can add three others, but I want to fill out their meaning in the next chapter: 'Webtrembler', 'Cairnbuilder', and 'Presbyter': all five I've puzzled my way towards, partly to indicate on my headed notepaper something of who I am and what I do . But I do not know what particular new name I might be given. I think I have been living with the kind of experience that can lead any of us to *choose* a new name (as some people do at

Confirmation, or on joining a community, or on a radical change of lifestyle) to add to our ancestral surname and our name *given* by parents. I am not sure it qualifies me yet to receive a new name, *given* by 'God'.

❖

FORGETTING AND REMEMBERING   To think about memory is to be perplexed by something strange. It has disturbed me to reflect on having no memory of much of the worst days of my illness. Certainly this book could not have been written without the memories of others filling in the gaps of my forgetting.

We all have impaired memories. Someone said there are three advantages of a bad memory: you dare not lie, you can enjoy the same story more than once. And – er – I've forgotten the third.

One of you out there thought of both nostalgia and depression as selective and protective devices to screen out unpleasant memories. Certainly, what we sometimes think are memories are but the products of overheated fantasy. Also this: if we are caught up in any event, we experience more than any film could show. The visual record is one-directional, often only two-dimensional, only one person's view. It may nudge other memories, which are in turn selective. For example, music may be played on 'authentic' instruments, from the eighteenth or nineteenth centuries, but it is played by turn-of-the-twenty-first-century musicians and heard by turn-of-the-twenty-first-century ears.

Add to the fact that we ordinarily forget most of what happens on any one day. We can think about something else while going through routines. We make a joke about our car or bicycle; it could find its way blindfold. We reflect what was going on in our minds, not what we saw in front of our eyes.

❖

I have been able to recall some of the 'trivia' of my time in hospital, though I have resisted the process. For there is much that I do not want to remember, nor need to remember. But I have very little or no memory of the worst of my distress, either the paralysis or the rage. I do not consciously remember giving up the will to live. I know that my forgetfulness is partly due to drugs and partly to the sessions of ECT. Are these events totally beyond recall? Does the use of anaesthetics involve a merciful but irrevocable amnesia? Has the adult experience of paralysis and rage, terror and despair, been necessary as a recovery of repressed memory, only to be forgotten because of the interventions of medicine? Do they need to surface again to be integrated or has my body, my being, become sufficiently aware even without my ability consciously to recall those feeling events? I am certainly more easily able in daily life to feel grief and fear and anger; there is the motion of e-motion at work, the shuddering of tears, the trembling of fear, the surge of anger. But they can come, it seems from nowhere, from what has been forgotten, out of proportion as responses to current events, tending towards an outpouring that no longer *sees* what is going on. Again, it is all a deeper mystery than I ever knew. Tread carefully. Here be dragons still, or landmines that may not yet have been defused. My journey still involves visits to the cellar, but in freedom and with companions, so that what is still locked away may come into the light of day, no longer to affect me and others harmfully.

At the same time I have to beware of making total recall and integration into an idol. Bless the broken ... Bless the fragments ... Bless the mess. Bless the forgetting, for the remembrance of accumulated pain, if exploding into consciousness too soon and all at once, can destroy.

And there is always forgiveness, for the mistakes you made, even when there was no ill will, for overwhelming presence out of mixed motives, for treatments with unwanted side

effects, for fearful withdrawals because my distress made
your half-forgotten demons stir in their sleep. There is
much more in the open than there used to be. There are
memories that have lost their power to harm. Forgiveness
has helped to dissolve the pain and has helped in the process
of forgetting. Hatchets can be buried – and the map of their
location burnt. Because the power of the memory to distort
the present is no longer blind in its rage, it can be let go of:
it is simply not there any more. The slate has indeed been
washed clean.

There is much in our corporate memory as a nation that we
cannot yet forgive and forget. There is much that is too raw,
there are too many memories of loss. The desire for
vengeance still festers. The wounds of wars are still open.
The dynamic of superiority and scapegoating that can treat
others as subhuman is still far too alive and well. My personal experience of these last three years has helped me further to take to myself these truths, until all the ambiguities
of forgetting and remembering seem like a Victorian minia-
ture, or a manageable and accurate microcosm of what happens on a larger scale among the peoples of the world.

I think this is why I had a deep desire to preach on
Remembrance Sunday last year, twisting the arm of a long
suffering friendly vicar to let me do so. It was the first time
since falling ill that I had given a sermon. It took a long time
to prepare, so involved did I become, so aware of the matching of themes. So I end this chapter, not with what I said exactly but with the extended manuscript which was too long
for an address but from which its substance was taken.

Rudyard Kipling's 'If' is the nation's favourite poem,
according to a BBC poll. It matches a quiet and modest
remembrance, no longer glorifying in war, perpetuating no
militaristic pomp, rather bringing to mind and heart again

the small deeds of courage, the supreme sacrifice, comradeship in arms, "greater love hath no man than this ... ", the choice of the lesser evil of war in the face of the greater evil of fascist domination and imperialism, and gratitude that such evils have been contained these past fifty years at lesser cost.

That is one vital element of any act of Remembrance. But I am bound to ask. Is the picture complete? What else might need to be placed in the frame – lest we forget ... ?

Lower down the poll of the nation's favourite poems, 29th I think, is one that is more uncomfortable than 'If': 'Anthem for Doomed Youth', written by Wilfred Owen in 1917. I think it is one of the greatest poems written in the English language this century. Its implications suggest a more rigorous remembrance than anything by Kipling, disturbing the calm waters of the noble and heroic appeal with cold winds of pain and anger, pity and warning:

> What passing-bells for these who die as cattle?
> Only the monstrous anger of the guns.
> Only the stuttering rifles' rapid rattle
> Can patter out their hasty orisons.
> No mockeries now for them; no prayers nor
>   bells,
> Nor any voice of mourning save the choirs, –
> The shrill, demented choirs of wailing shells;
> And bugles calling for them from sad shires.
> What candles may be held to speed them all?
> Not in the hands of boys, but in their eyes
> Shall shine the holy glimmers of goodbyes.
> The pallor of girls' brows shall be their pall;
> Their flowers the tenderness of patient minds,
> And each slow dusk a drawing-down of blinds.

❖

We would do especially well to let that opening line interrogate us as the leaves of autumn fall, are gathered, and burned in their millions:

"What passing-bells for these *who die as cattle*?"

(It is ironic that it is the cattle themselves who are bellow-
ing an accusing Last Post as the century ends.)

But let the question be put to the whole of this century as
we ask, What should we remember?

First: We have been caught up in rather more than a
century of mass production, of an industrial and economic process in which most human beings have been factory
'hands' who have been dispensed with whenever the
winds of market forces change direction – human beings
treated as commodities to be bought and sold, with little
control over their own lives, so often little more than serf
or slave.

Think too of the vast number of agricultural labourers
who went from giving fodder to the cattle to themselves becoming fodder for the guns and shells of Flanders –
weapons made by their cousins in mass producing factories
across the Channel. As one commentator on the Great War
put it, "Being shelled is the main work of the infantry soldier." And so they died – as cattle. (Thus Geoffrey Dyer
remembers in a most thoughtful book about that war, *The
Missing of the Somme*.)

Second: We have lived in a century of expanding bureau-
cracies. Our national insurance numbers render superfluous
the siren call for identity cards. We are all digitalized and
quantified now. By PIN or by letters of a password we have
access to numbers shifted around on a screen, trapped at
which are the office 'hands', taught by rote to conduct conversations with us, the bank's customers, almost entirely in
numbers. My attempts at banter on the telephone occasionally evoke a human response, but usually throw Tracy or
Wayne off course. I suppose this bit of bureaucracy is benign, but I sometimes feel as if I am drowning in a sea of
megabytes. And I cannot help remembering – indeed I am
convinced I am *required* to remember – the numbers branded on the arms of prisoners in the concentration camps,

much like the marks of ownership on cattle, nor the fact that many of Europe's Jews were transported to those camps in *cattle* trucks, the orders for both having been given by a demonic bureaucracy.

Here is Wilfred Owen again, a couple of pages on from his 'Anthem for Doomed Youth', from a poem called 'The Send-Off':

> Then, unmoved, signals nodded, and a lamp
> Winked to the guard.
>
> So secretly, like wrongs hushed-up, they went.
> They were not ours:
> We never heard to which front these were sent ...
>
> Shall they return to beatings of great bells
> In wild train-loads?
> A few, a few, too few for drums and yells,
> May creep back, silent, to still village wells
> Up half-known roads.

When I first read that, I thought for a moment that Owen was writing about the Jews, the words and images fit so well. But of course he is writing a generation before, and pictures the soldiers leaving England for an unknown destination. Both soldiers and Jews were to die as cattle.

Third: Given that so many human beings have been reduced to a 'hand' or a 'number' it is hardly a surprise that propaganda has not needed to be very sophisticated when comparing 'us' with 'them'. The enemy is easily thought of as subhuman. Ask this: Who is it that the opinion-moulders label as 'beast' or' fiend', or the 'dirty' ripe for 'cleansing'? Do that, and there is no compunction about killing them as cattle: for subhuman is what they have become in our eyes.

We need to be ever-vigilant. 'Fear of the foreigner' is a tune being played again by Little Englanders. And how many of us have protested against – or even been aware of

– our own little bit of – ahem – ethnic 'tidying up' of the green fields of England? Local authorities, with government and wider European backing, are no longer obliged to make the customary provisions for travelling people as will enable them to continue unharrassed their centuries-old way of life. Do not forget that, categorized as 'gypsies' they too were 'herded' into the camps of the Third Reich.

Remember too that a considerable number of the mentally handicapped were 'eliminated' in Hitler's Germany, imperfect specimens alongside the posters of the young perfectly formed Aryans.

Again, if to a lesser degree, and by default and neglect rather than by systematic ill will, England is not blameless. What stories of alienation, of an unwillingness to see, lie behind a simple inscription on the gate of a field a few miles to the west of Leeds, to the effect that the remains of nearly three thousand people are interred there, patients from the nearby High Royds Hospital: there are no names and no headstones, and slates are missing from the roof of what was once the cemetery chapel ...

We need all the help we can get if we are to answer Wilfred Owen's question. Of particular importance in that task is the book *If This is a Man*, by Primo Levi, an Italian Jewish chemist who survived Auschwitz and later wrote of his experiences there. This is part of the Preface:

> Many people – many nations – can find themselves holding, more or less wittingly, that 'every stranger is an enemy'. For the most part this conviction lies deep down like some latent injection; it betrays itself only in random, disconnected acts, and does not lie at the base of a system of reason. But when this does come about, when the unspoken dogma becomes the major premise in a syllogism, then, at the end of the chain, there is the Lager. Here is a product of a conception of the world carried rigorously

> to its logical conclusion. So long as the concep-
> tion subsists, the conclusion remains to threaten
> us. The story of the death camps should be un-
> derstood by everyone as a sinister alarm-signal.

No, there are never any passing bells, only alarm-bells, for those who die as cattle, the mark of the Beast indeed 'upon their arms'.

Fourth: Along with this categorizing of the stranger as the enemy, there is another temptation. To a century of in- creasing and bewildering complexity we all too easily react by *simplifying*.

Think of the claims of superiority made by the so-called racially pure over against the complex reality of human mongrels. Think of the claims of superiority made by the sexually and genetically sound over against the complex reality of human diversity. Think of the slogans, always cheap, usually nasty, that deny the rich variety of rainbow humanity.

Think of the strident trumpeting of 'family' values which scapegoat the mother with three children whose husband has left her and who finds herself treated as a moral deviant by her church.

Think of the ways in which *you* were brought up to feel superior and to stigmatize other groups of people as inferior – and think of the ways in which you know yourself stigmatized, whether visibly or hidden. Too easily do we lock the stigmatized away, if only in a hidden corner of our minds and refuse the effort of *connecting* with them. It is so easy to settle into a cosy amnesia.

Think again of those groups stigmatized by Nazi Germany – Jews above all, and gypsies, homosexuals, Jehovah's Witnesses, political dissidents, migrant workers. Ask yourself, how many people from amongst those 'cate- gories' do you count among your *friends*?

I press the question on myself: brought up with the 'obvious' advantage of being a boy and not a girl; superior

to most of humankind as a member of the master race that
'humanely' ruled a quarter of the globe; speaking the language that of course God and St.Paul spoke; educated at the
best school in town and at one of the two universities that
constituted the most powerful closed shop in the country;
taught, however subtly, that the words Catholic, Jew, and
homosexual were not neutral descriptions but laden with
hostile meaning. Mostly we didn't talk about these things,
nor did we draw too close. "God bless Uncle Jack and his
room-mate Harry whom we're not supposed to talk about."
In none of these ways of feeling superior did the church of
my youth suggest we were betraying the Gospel and dis-
obeying God.

So: hands, numbers, beasts, fiends, inferior, subhuman,
impure, unclean. Add to that brew economic uncertainty
and political insecurity, and none of us who inherit the
weight of European history is far from the fury that cries
Havoc, and lets slip the dogs of war.

And in this year 1996?

One quarter of the people of France, Italy, and Austria
support very right wing political parties which should be
named as fascist ...

A memorial to the Jews of Vienna – 190,000 in 1938,
6000 today – was due to be erected this month in the heart
of the city's Jewish quarter. A petition signed by 2000 other
citizens has, at least temporarily, blocked it. They do not
want that *reminder* in their midst ...

Rachel Clark comments in *The Guardian*: " ... those determined to conceal history ... collude with those who
know nothing about it." Like a certain footballer giving the
Nazi salute during a game: he said he did but jest ...

And a small incident in a family. My cousin's husband has
a responsible job with an international shipping company.
They were telling me that his employer was tight-fisted and
had been mean with provisions at last year's office

Christmas party. They also said he was Jewish. Why? It was hardly necessary, and it ignored the history of generous hospitality shown by Jewish families. And I wasn't quick-witted enough to say, with a wink, Good job he isn't Scottish ...

❖

If you are familiar with the bells round the necks of cows browsing in Alpine pastures, remember there were no passing-bells for those who died as cattle.

❖

And heed the warning of the Czech novelist Kundera who wrote that "humanity's struggle against (coercive) power is memory's struggle against oblivion."

❖

Do not, then, keep *your* memories to yourself both good and bad, of war. Endure the pain and sorrow of telling your story to those of us who have no memories. Let not the war in Burma be 'forgotten'.

Let ordinary people tell their stories of doing their ordinary bit, who rose above the monotony of their work, their feelings of being but a number, their sense of stigma. *Stories* are always unique, and by them we cherish our humanity.

And let the young ask those who are older, gently but insistently, to have the courage to tell their stories, that they may be not forgotten.

Courage is indeed needed if it is to be the *whole* story, not merely the selective parts easily remembered today. Let the truths we tell not be partial. For Europe is still not far from the slaughter of those who die as cattle.

❖

So remember that the glory of war perished for ever in the mud of the Somme on the first of July 1916 ...

Remember that the military mind will, *in extremis*, use *any* means towards an end thought justifiable ...

Remember that organizational failure is always partially covered up by tales of individual courage and bravery. I was brought up on the shining example of Scott of the Antarctic (and later on one of his good companions, Edward Wilson, still a hero for his faith, unselfishness, scientific dedication, and artistic skill). But I have to recognize now that on that fatal expedition to the South Pole, "a virtue was made of calamity and incompetence was dressed up as heroism." So too was the Great War ...

Remember, with Elaine Scarry that "the main purpose and outcome of war is injury", however 'necessary' a conflict may have become when other means of resolution failed ...

Remember that the memorials of war become neglected, sprayed with graffiti, chipped by vandals, smoothed by pollution, the very name fading. Who now salutes the Crimean War Memorial in the botanical gardens along the road? Jewish gravestones are desecrated anew with swastikas by the young who do not sense they belong, and whose harsh faces qualify them as recruits for the work of camp guards ...

Remember those who died as cattle ...

Owen's question presses us further, but with a different emphasis, presses particularly on those who call themselves Christian.

"What *passing-bells* for those who die as cattle?"

The quick answer is none. Mass deaths, unmarked graves, unknown so-called 'resting' places, corpses drifting down to the ocean floor, ashes to dust, even a human body reduced in a fraction of a second to a black shadow across a pavement in Hiroshima. Nothing is left to bury, not even to scatter. Nothing is left of the ordered, timely, personal and corporate rites of burial and mourning.

And there have been so *many*. The deaths of Auschwitz and Hiroshima provoke dumb horror. There is no poetry in response. And Christian faith is at best in suspension, and for most a discarded failure.

Think first of Auschwitz: We do not know what a truly *Christian* faith would be like if we really embraced (rather than tried to extinguish) our brothers and sisters with whom we share a common father, Abraham. There is so much penitence to be done, so much reconciliation to be sought.

Ever since the Christian Church has exercised political power, it has committed, or colluded with the committing of, fratricide against Jews and Muslims. Into the moral vacuum left by a retreating sea of faith stepped the policy of genocide. Even the New Testament has misled us. The earliest Gospels were written by and for *Christian* Jews to convince other *Jews*, i.e. Pharisee Jews, Sadducee Jews, Essene Jews, Zealot Jews, that Jesus was the Messiah. By the time of the Gospel of John, *Gentile* Christians were arguing against *all* Jews, and a religious argument *between* Jews became religious hostility *against* Jews. Add political power, from the fourth century onwards, and pogroms begin. Sacred Scriptures are used to promote atrocities and murder. As always, we should be, as so often we are not, *very* careful in our handling of the Scriptures. Knowing what we now know, we must dare to say that Jesus is betrayed, however unintentionally, by those who wrote about him.

If Auschwitz urges a new exploration of how much we owe, in penitence to the Jews and in gratitude for the Jews, Hiroshima urges us to think again about how we understand 'resurrection'. Again, we have to handle Scriptures very carefully. We are given stories of a risen Jesus who ate fish and invited touch, from which grew a theology of the resurrection of the *flesh*, based on a biology which thought the bone at the base of the spine (aptly called the sacrum) was indestructible, and went on to say that it would be from that bone that the resurrection body would grow.

Tell that to the family of the black shadow of Hiroshima or of the ovens of Auschwitz. In any case, that old belief is nonsense. *Nothing* remains that is *recognizably* of the unique you or me. Further, in the opinion of Dominic Crossan, *nothing* of even the corpse of Jesus remained. Stories were woven later about his burial to give him honour: crucifixion was scandalous enough, a corpse left to the vultures and the wild dogs was too much. Roman punishment, whether by wild beasts, burning, or crucifixion, *included* the social *shame* of there being no burial. But shame would be consistent for the Jesus of scandal. Very human to add a tomb, then a respected follower of influence, then two, then a garden, then an excess of spices and ointment. But much more likely historically is the horror and the shame, characteristic of countless deaths since.

Resurrection faith is in the God who creates out of *nothing* and loves those who in the eyes of others are already as nothing, nonentities and nobodies, the very 'hands', the 'numbers', and the 'subhuman' who died as cattle.

They died as cattle. There were no passing-bells. We live through a dark night of faith. All we have are our wounds and our stories. And yes, we want to forget so much of what happens in war, we cannot bear to remember. We want 'each slow dusk' to be 'a drawing down of blinds', blinds that conceal and help us to forget. But hidden wounds fester. Truths written out of the record come back to haunt. Rather keep the wounds exposed to the air: only by weeping can they begin to heal, and even in time become, as Julian of Norwich saw, 'worships'. Scars that witness to an unexpected trans-figuration – that too is profound truth proclaimed by resurrection story. O that Christian and Jew together could feel safe enough to share the stories of their wounds, caused by war and by religion.

Let us together lament and cry, God, why have you forsaken us? And this keening question, How long, O Lord, how long? And let us together hear God's questions to us, My people, what have I done to you? And this, What is your *name*? (What are you really like, now?)

As bodies weep and touch again, as bread again is broken and shared, the indestructible Spirit of Love will take shape among us in new and glorious ways, deeper than the deepest wounds, and more real than ash or shadow. The passing bells will call to deeper prayer and a greater rejoicing, and in the fields there will be an abundance, even of cattle.

V

Breezes

CAUTIOUSLY ALERT   You would not let me get into the boat without a life-jacket on. You watched anxiously as I edged beyond the harbour wall for the first time, you my trustworthy tugs of such varied shapes and appearances ...

You may have needed a coat of paint, but you looked cheerful and weather-beaten ...

You certainly knew these waters well and you were never really afraid; you probably hoodwinked a coastguard or two from time to time ...

You preferred to work to a timetable, and you had got used to ferrying tourists and locals across the harbour, never having been one for anything remotely like the high seas ...

Yours was the quietest engine, the most discreet paintwork and lettering, looked up to with a little envy by some of the others ...

And still I have company, some with the nautical skills I had always thought I had but did not. I am learning to read the charts, understand the shipping forecast better, listen to the ancient lore of those who mend nets and gossip while they do, watch more closely for nature's danger signals.

I have chosen warm waters to test out my boat after its long refit, Greek Islands rather than Outer Hebrides, early summer rather than late autumn. There is a fresh breeze blowing. I begin to relax, to look around me again, to hear wise voices in neighbouring boats, to discover some new perspectives. To my surprise, I had been aware of most of them before, and had even written some of them down as the squall was beginning to gather. But I was moving so fast, so busily, that I had not given them the time and attention they required.

Some of what I have been learning has come from recordings of wind song, birdsong, wavesong, from distant shores and waters. I am reminded also of Kierkegaard's metaphor of faith as launching out on the sea, with a thousand fathoms below.

❖

A LEAKING VALVE   Of course, I want to make *sense* of it all. And of course, I shall never be able to. I am comforted, though, by a gloss on the story of Moses' encounter with God. When asked his name, God is reported to have replied, "I Am That I Am." "What's that supposed to mean?" Moses responds somewhat truculently. "It doesn't make sense." God's riposte is in the grand tradition of Jewish humour, "When have I ever promised you I would make sense?"

Once in a while, though, I have come across reports from the wilderness of the vast ocean, and they have helped me to know that I am not completely on my own, indeed that others know the seascape far better than I ever shall. I have sometimes recognized the configurations they describe. For example, this extract from a letter by David Sargeant in the *Eremos* magazine gave me hope that what I had been through was not only a biochemical frenzy:

> So, say Bergson (and Aldous Huxley and Rayor Johnson) the main function of the brain is to narrow down the cosmic consciousness to the biological awareness necessary for survival. The brain is the valve of the mind.
>
> But the valve can sometimes leak. Certain drugs, diseases, injuries etc. can cause the efficiency of the brain to falter, and allow some of this cosmic Mind-at-Large to get through. In someone unprepared for this, the experience

overwhelms the mind and the person suffers
what we call a mental breakdown ...
... some types of Altered States of Consciousness are destructive, others therapeutic,
and still others of great spiritual value.

Or, I would want to claim, all three. I am still amazed to
realize that the entries in my journal in the spring of 1994,
however reduced to hasty scribbles some of them were, gave
me the substance of what was going to take a very long time
to absorb and begin to use. In retrospect, I can see that far
too much was happening far too quickly, and because I did
not pause, take time to do nothing, to rest and to be, the
squall and the doldrums were the only course left, emergency action that so nearly proved fatal.

PRIVILEGE AND PAIN   You startled me when you said that
what I had experienced was a privilege. I should have been
used to your gnomic sayings by then, but it took me a while
to register the considerable grain of truth. Compared with
most people in the world, I have time and energy beyond
what I need for survival. I have been able to spend much of
that 'spare' in explorations of various kinds, taking both
outer and inner journeys, however unpredictable some of
them have been. And increasingly I have been able to make
a living outside the usual conventions of labels and institutional roles. You too thought that too much bliss had come
my way: the container could not handle it and was severely
damaged. (Watch the dosage in future – and do not luxuri-
ate in your 'Stigmata': victims can be their own worst ene-
mies.) ECT restored my brain patterns to so-called normal,
but there is still chaos to be faced that those around me
could not sit with. How much 'madness' is intuition un-
heard and unconnected?

But there are other things to be said in order to keep that
notion of privilege in perspective. Pain is still pain, and

there is compassion as well as fear in our response of wanting to reduce it. Emergency measures were taken for my *survival;* only later was there the luxury of breathing space to look into what I needed for my future well-being. Pain can be destructive, not enlightening, and I am grateful for the action that was taken to lessen my distress.

Actually, pain is too general a word to use; dislocation, turmoil, distress, anxiety, restlessness, bewilderment, the physical symptoms of grief and fear and rage, terror at an approaching needle to take a blood test, despair, and the sense of the *waste* of all that time ...

In truth we are usually far from bliss – or what we are going through makes us think we are. We are living at a time of ever extending purgatories. More and more people are living with various notes of pain which cannot yet be woven into melody, more like a hideous drawn out screech on gut. We are living, enduring, a lot longer than we did in the days before sophisticated medical procedures. And we make courageous attempts to 'live' for years with HIV, with cancers, with fatigue syndromes, and we can continue to 'exist' for years with dementia, with the aftermath of accidents that leave us in comas, or of shocks that have blown minds and bodies apart. Do not ask me to make *sense* of all that. But I do have a desire for accurate knowledge, keen discernment, and boundless compassion as we human beings try to come to terms with the ethical dilemmas our discoveries and skills have brought to us.

❖

FEAR I have often wondered if they are right, those who have suggested, usually enigmatically, that we are more afraid of joy than we are of pain. Afraid to let go of control, we seize up in shock. Afraid of love, we settle for calculation and comfort.

Is it true that when I was frighteningly ill, there were few people who had faced enough of their own fear to be at ease with mine? Were they actually more afraid than I was, or

more afraid than I at the time was aware of being afraid of?
And how often do I suddenly become conscious of holding
my breath, of going stiff – minor versions of the rigidity of
terror that can kill quicker than starvation?

In Pat Barker's trilogy about the First World War and the
early days of psychiatric medicine, she has her character Dr
Rivers (a psychiatrist who was actually practising near
Edinburgh at the time) say that "the quantity of neurotic
symptoms" in soldiers "correlated not with the intensity of
battle, the length of an individual's service, or his emotional predisposition, but with the degree of his *immobility*."
(My italics)

It is no use trying to crack fear open: that leads only to
worse rigidity, trapped as you are between the impossibili-
ties of flight or fight. Courage, trust, love – big words for
the small gentle melting acts that are needed – can do some
healing work, taking the sting ever so slowly out of the
common fears we all have, of the cold, of pain, of the darkness, and perhaps of those exceptional fears too, the traumas
of violation. But it takes longer than I have yet given to that
process to be able to live these sensible words of John
Macmurray:

> The maxim of illusory religious runs: 'Fear not,
> trust in God and he will see that none of the
> things you fear will happen to you;' that of real
> religion, on the contrary is: 'Fear not, the things
> you are afraid of are quite likely to happen to
> you, but they are nothing to be afraid of.'

REALITY   John Macmurray was passionate about what is
real in religion. Only with that in mind could I agree with
an Australian poet who wrote, "Depression is what you get
when you are not religious." For one of my friends his ministry in psychiatric hospitals had been motivated by the
desire to strip away delusions, ego, fantasy, to ask what is

really, *truly*, going on in what is going on. The *swollen* ego, *puffed* up by pride (and the rest), the bloated and inflated self, has to be 'punctured' by 'compunction'. (There is of course the opposite falsehood, that we are of no worth and deserve to be doormats.) We need to see the world and ourselves as they really are. Without this, religion does become a matter of the delusions built up by games of power, and is nearly always characterized by romanticism and sentimentality (love out of true) and the opposite side of the same coin – coldness and cruelty (power out of true).

Indeed, I had become perilously 'out of true', out of touch with my real being, my *embodied* being, my deeper self, indeed too isolated for my own good. And with the death of my mother I had lost touch with the primal physical source of my being, the cutting of a cord that for a second time left me 'all at sea'.

And a culture that has lost touch with touch was the context for your ironic remark that as a heterosexual visitor from overseas you had been in this country a month before you were warmly embraced, by two people from sexual minorities who have had to learn from scratch what touch is about, but as a result are often more relaxed at hugging their heterosexual friends than those latter are with one another!

So the process of healing has involved learning again half-forgotten and neglected lessons of touch, through which I am *really* present to you and you to me: loving and accurate touch of course, but more than a message and a word. The touch of a hand at ease with itself, the embrace that lingers a second or two beyond mere courtesy, and the vibrations of a voice down the telephone: these were all confirmations of these words of Oliver Sacks:

> … reality is given to us by the reality of people; our sense of reality, of trust or security, is critically dependent on a human relation. A single good relation is a lifeline [that] can extricate

[patients] from trouble. Friendship is healing;
we are physicians to each other.

Even with that help, in the company of a person very real
to me, I can still pull over myself "a thin coverlet of talk",
hoping to make the other feel comfortable by pretending I
am in better shape than I really [sic] am. I still need to pay
honest attention to myself.

That quoted phrase was by Anne Truitt, from a letter to,
and referred to by, May Sarton. She goes on to praise
Rembrandt for

> painting himself as he knew himself, human
> being beyond reprieve. He looks out from this
> position, without self-pity and without flourish,
> and lends me strength.

I rather agree with May Sarton's envy of the painter who
does not have to use "elusive, sometimes damaged, often
ambivalent *words*".

Help me in my search for reality. Be real, really yourself,
really present, with me. And shine a torch on me that I may
see myself as I truly am.

WEB TREMBLING   I am more than ever convinced that the
whole is greater than the sum of the parts, and that the
whole of us – couple, family, tribe, whatever – is greater
than the sum of the individuals concerned. The different
parts of me are intimately connected, and we are all as
human beings deeply inter-connected.

I am grateful that the portion of the psychiatric world
where my lot fell was not reductionist. I was not seen sole-
ly in terms of biochemistry and electricity. The disorder,
disruption, and disintegration that was threatening to over-
whelm me – these were all recognized – *and* that it was the
unique I who was suffering. Nor was my illness interpreted

in terms of an alien malignant force that had to be cut out or expelled. As Oliver Sacks puts it:

> Diseases have a character of their own, but they also partake of our character; we have a character of our own, but we also partake of the world's character ... the disease, the person, the world go together, and cannot be considered separately as things-in-themselves.

Thus part of the interconnectedness is as part of a world gone wrong; the web can tremble with disease and distortion as well as with health and truth. The corporate body of which I have been most connected is that of the Church, happily insofar as 'she' is a living organism from which came much love and wisdom in my direction, less happily insofar is 'it' is a patriarchal and hierarchical institution distorted by the misusings of power and which is only beginning to allow women and gay people to move more freely within it. I had been caught up in the inevitable stresses of exclusion and isolation, so much so that I had become far too familiar with lack of support, being so used to it that I did not think it dangerous to neglect those willing to give me critical and helpful solidarity. And those on the edge do lose out financially, unprotected by the securities of the system. It is so easy to inch your way along a branch, becoming more visible the further out you go from the trunk, be admired for your audacity as an innovator, but unaware until it is too late that the branch is about to crack.

To speak and write critically of the power games visible in the architecture and organization of the churches and audible in the language of its prayers, of the historical record on matters of human sexuality, of the image, practice and theology of the ordained ministry, all these have gained me friends but no favours. I would not want to be doing anything else, it is satisfying and sometimes exhilarating work. But it has the costs of isolation – occasional serious misjudgements, defensiveness about those in authority, feelings of alienation at regular standard Sunday worship, exclusion from places of decision, a stress that threatens sanity.

Add to this the pressures towards an unhealthy degree of privacy if you are gay, even if you have a partner. There is rapid change now, but the climate of my earlier years said, "Better not to do it at all, but if you must, hide it behind locked doors." Relationships that are cut off from neighbourly social intercourse can all too easily turn in on themselves. We all thrive with the support and teasing of our friends, our colleagues, our fellow believers. This is not to decry appropriate privacies; it is to criticize those who are fearful and cannot at the very least marginally *include* what they find unusual.

By contrast, then, I find myself tearfully moved as I think of the way in which the web of my rare 'extended family' did tremble for my good – however much the more distant 'cousins' did not even know of one another's existence. A Christmas card I received had this prayer: "Lord I am at the end of my tether. I pray that you are at the other end." Well, Mysterious and Puzzling One, through your representative and long-suffering friends, I guess you were!

To realize I was a cell of a living organism was to learn that I could receive as well as give. In the state I was in I could do no other. But it was guilt-relieving to recognize that I did not have to expend any energy in praying. I could let others do that on my behalf.

You pointed out to me that the words of prayer which I had shaped in some of my books had helped others to pray. While these were not exactly credit in a spiritual bank, they might have been used so that some energy came back to me to undergird me. I am touched by that thought – and awed again at how we influence one another without knowing it.

I recalled the story in the Gospels when the friends of a paralyzed man dug a hole in the roof to let him down on his pallet in front of Jesus who was hemmed in by a crowd of people. "Seeing *their* faith" he healed the man (Mark 2.5).

At the very least their contribution seems to have been a trigger. Who knows what was worked in me through others who were 'praying' for me? I had no will of my own, little awareness of what was happening, no skills in my own cause. Was other people's energy flowing into me when I had none of my own, a sort of spiritual blood transfusion? Are we all, fine tuned to the wavelengths of the 'spiritual body', almost tangibly in connection?

Another of the triggers making some of this possible may well have been my 'confessions', my anxious, almost compulsive, telling of truths I usually keep to myself, the darker side of me, whatever degrees of blame may or may not have been appropriate. I had to wipe my own slate clean – or rather write on it and trust others to do the cleaning, to release me from the burden of guilt. I was also dependent on their not using what I said against me: I had put power in their hands: would they show mercy? That done, was there even more energy from others available for my healing? We forget how isolating it is, how distancing those who love us find it, if we cover ourselves "from head to foot in a shining impermeable condom of irreproachable behaviour". (That comes from another letter to May Sarton, by Sylvia Townsend Warner.) And that barrier to the touch of skin against skin has been removed, to the possibility of new life.

So much of what passes for prayer is an attempt to twist God's arm, to manipulate the strings of a heavenly puppeteer. You told me that when you were staying in my house while I was in hospital, your 'prayer' was to think of me, to reflect on my situation, and to seek appropriate decisions and actions, as accurately, truthfully, and lovingly as possible (which included keeping people away from me!). You resisted the temptation to use prayer as a therapeutic technique for yourself in trying to adjust yourself to the shock of what had happened, to tell God exactly what you wanted (and you may well have reckoned God owed you one after all the hours you had put in over the years ...), to

seek a specific outcome that would make life more comfortable for you.

I find myself still mightily puzzled. If we were to expect
our prayers to be effective in proportion to their quantity,
the most whole and saintly person in this country should be
the Queen. I am moved by the thought of so many people
praying for me while I was ill, humbled by the fact that not
only did the sun never set on the British Empire (!), it did
not set on prayers for Jim. It was an outpouring of love,
often feeling frustrated at its helplessness, but genuine and
caring. But the more of it, the greater the effect?

I find myself thinking of such prayer as our aligning our
wills, our minds, our love with God's, seeking to be the trigger that will release the flow of that love in the world.
Perhaps I can think of myself as a sluice-gate. But both
'trigger' and 'sluice-gate' are impersonal metaphors and do
not do justice to my humanity. If God is *not* a puppeteer, *not*
an impersonal force, but a supra-human reality who acts
personally, and in free and considered response, rather than
in automatic reaction, then my contribution is vital. It cannot of itself *make* the giving of blessing happen, but it is an
integral part of its happening, and the gift cannot be given
without it.

Whatever the 'how' of whatever 'it' was – and we have to
live with unanswerable questions – I am grateful 'it' was
going on. Connections held, not least I believe through the
praying of solitaries, in that paradox of the life of hermits
who, though physically alone, know themselves to be deeply
in solidarity with nature and with humankind, solidly together in God. They become acutely aware of the struggle
with those dense and heavy strands of energy that try and
choke the life out of the lighter more fragile strands. Again
we can but use metaphors, but the struggles of good against
evil *are* real, the striving to transform pain and darkness, or
if not transform, to lessen it, to quieten it. The hermit, solitary, supported by the twin pillars of silence and simplicity
so as not to be entangled in noise and clutter, becomes an

acute point of exchange, a power house of praying. A few of them held me to themselves-in-God in the eye of the storm. Maybe they kept me – and keep the world – from disintegration.

These convictions about our being so puzzlingly and often invisibly connected are not new. But they have become stronger this far side of the squall, more finely honed, more securely embodied. I must still beware of letting my head and my words run off in front of me: I do not want the living organism that is Jim to collapse again under the strain.

Yet again I am astonished to look back at some notes of a sermon I preached at the beginning of the month when I fell ill.

I began by talking of the folly of the preacher, the wordsmith, who dares to use inadequate and broken words to speak of the Mystery of Love whom some call God. I referred to the time and effort it takes to craft words. Why did I do it? To make sense of my life – a foolish task as I have already hinted, yet always being attempted, even when success can never be more than partial. That was one answer. Another was out of a desire to pray in words that make prayer authentic for me now, that are in my own voice. That does not mean that I intentionally use bizarre and idiosyncratic words, but that I try to find language that has bite and that others may recognize and adapt to their own use. When I discovered that more than a few people were being helped by their eavesdropping, I had the temerity to publish them, becoming a freelance entrepreneur in the God business, maybe even aided and abetted by my greengrocer and company secretary grandfathers!

I further set the scene by describing the folly of saying Yes to other people's requests to be their 'godfriend' – soulfriend if you like. In conversation, the one is asking the other to be a discerning listener to words and gestures and silences, to bear their burdens for a while, and to explore the question of what is really going on in what is going on in their lives – in their illness, their bereavement, their sexuality, their work, their ministry. Together we look for patterns, connections, directions, that give clues as to how their lives are being shaped by God.

This led me on to explore the significance of three small words we usually take for granted – 'for', 'from', 'in'.

For: It is Christian practice for me to try to put myself out for you, unconditionally, without hidden motives, purged of greed, possessiveness, and domination, whatever the cost. This is *agape.* It can degenerate into hard-edged duty, the kind of sacrifice that is characteristic of the unlovely and untouchable do-gooder. And I may well forget that you are also here to put yourself out for me. I have to give up the delusion that I can manage on my own. If I am unsure of being loved, of being accepted for and despite who I am, if I think myself of no worth, I may indeed compensate by so living for others that I avoid the need to face my own pain and ask for love for myself.

From: So it is a prior truth that I live *from* you. Who I am has been shaped by my interaction with you ... and you ... and you. I live from the gifts of others, from their attention to me, and from their engagement with me. My singularity, founded on my unique combination of genes, is built from countless interactions with the 'others' in my life.

If you are twenty and I am fifty, I shall be dependent on gifts from you in my old age, including your hard work to earn enough money to pay taxes, some of which may subsidize my bus pass and railcard. Interdependence is fundamental to our survival and flourishing. We live by exchange: *for* one another, *from* one another.

Is it an old saying, "Neighbour's shopping bag lighter

than own shopping bag"? Washing up at a friend's house always feels less of a chore than at home. Sharing the load lightens it. It is lighter for the host who has one less routine to do, lighter for the guest, for whom it is a simpler task than at home. And potential friendships can be tested further, away from the intensity of looking at each other.

More profoundly, we cannot save, heal, help ourselves. There was a deep truth in the ironic taunt thrown at the crucified Jesus, "He saved others; himself he cannot save." (I know that was a rueful reflection of a few friends when I fell ill; ironic indeed that I should have used it myself but a month or so earlier.)

I went on to draw attention to Charles Williams' novel, *Descent into Hell*, where one of the characters, Peter Stanhope, offers to 'carry' the fear that a Pauline Anstruther has of meeting her 'double' whom she has once encountered in terror. As she walks home, he sits in his chair and imagines himself walking where she is walking and feeling her fear coming on himself. "The body of his flesh received her alien terror, his mind carried the burden of her world. The burden was inevitably lighter for him than for her, for the rage of a personal resentment was lacking. He endured her sensitiveness, but not her sin; the substitution there, if indeed there is a substitution, is hidden in the central mystery of Christendom which Christendom itself has never understood, nor can." Meanwhile, Pauline has reached home without the terror coming upon her.

Substitution and exchange in the mysteries of evil, pain, and love: Charles Williams' favourite word is 'co-inherence': we bear one another's burdens, we belong to one another, and the truth of this inextricable connection is focused sharply and centrally on the life and work of Christ. It is the interpenetration of lives lived *from* one another and *for* one another.

In: The process is complete when we can *live* the truth – and

not merely claim and pro-claim it – that, with Paul, we are
'*in* Christ', with John, that Christ dwells, abides, lingers *in*
us and we *in* Christ. Mutual indwelling is the *heart* of it all,
the mirroring and imaging of the inner life of God as
Trinity, the mystery of each of three living, from, for, and in
the other, the original and ultimate holy communion.

So, if God dwells *in* us, if, that is, the Spirit, the Energy of
God is within us already, if we were to become fully awake
to that truth, we would know that there is in each of us an
infinite capacity to bear burdens. It would be folly in the
worst sense of the word for any of us to claim that this was
completely so: nevertheless the possibility is awesome and
the occasional practice humbling. It is the meaning of "Take
my yoke upon you: bearing the load with me is light." But
the bearing is in the power of a love not our own.

We belong together, 'incorporated' in an enterprise beyond the tensions of business competition; we can *never* be
separated. We can remain a very long time unaware of this
reality, we may isolate ourselves, we may be asleep, deathly
pale, in danger of perishing, or we may wake up to the truth
of who we really are. And we may believe that divine love
will wait for as long as it takes for us to waken, in the mean-
time bearing the burden in that ultimate exchange.

The implications are profound for faith and life now. If
we really belong together in a divine and human co-inherence, any claims to superiority over against others are at
best provisional and ultimately pale into insignificance. If
we examine the biblical record of the human encounter
with the living God, we notice a struggle between two in-
terpretations of that encounter. One is exclusive, restricting
God's love and favour to those who believe themselves specially chosen for privilege for the few, and are even convinced they are obeying God's will when they indulge in
'ethnic cleansing'. The other is inclusive, expanding God's
love and favour beyond those who believe themselves

specially chosen, to embrace and serve all people, who become convinced that they are obeying God's will when they are willing to be thought tainted by drawing close to the unclean. The conviction that "I am saved and you are damned" struggles with the conviction that "I can be saved only by you, by gift, by grace *from* you, that I may live *for* you and for others, all of us broken, all of us being healed, all belonging to one another." It is the truth that the fanatic and fundamentalist in each of us finds it hard to acknowledge, because we then have to own up to our insecurity: it can no longer be bolstered by the conviction that we can flourish only at the expense of others' downfall. The 'worldly' always prefer the easier, simpler ways of superiority and condemnation. It is a tough love that wakes us up to, and a tough discipline that keeps us awake to, the truth that only in bearing one another's burdens can we fulfil the law of Christ.

As I recall that sermon now, along with asides and illustrations, preached with confidence and conviction, I think ruefully that I did not recognize how prophetic it was for me. Three years on, the wordsmith is back in the smithy. Whether there is a different quality to what I will now write, whether I will discover a new genre, I do not yet know. Perhaps there will be more stories, more poetry; miniatures and signposts shaped from closer and longer attention to the everyday.

I was also aware, as the zephyrs fluttered the sails new hoisted for testing in the harbour, that the way I had to navigate still included this task :

In prayer I need to pay attention to the meaning(s) of the words. I know they can never fully, often barely adequately, express what is true. But I can take care that they are doing a modest job as signposts pointing in the right direction. The problem with so much of what we have inherited is that, even if they have not fallen down, they are now

pointing in the wrong direction, and so must be turned
round ...

The cost and the pleasure of attention ... biting the
words to test the worth of their currency ... sounding them
from my body ... speaking in my own voice, but even more
authentically with the authority of a survivor ... miniatures
... signposts ... stories ... laughter ... communicating ... in
communion ... the lightness of bearing ...

PUBLIC AND PRIVATE: SHOWMANSHIP AND SEXUALITY

Writing a fairly autobiographical book about an illness feels
a bit too nineties for comfort. A lot of people are doing it.
It feels parallel to being an ecclesiastical entrepreneur in the
climate of the eighties, encouraging as it was to the setting
up of small businesses. I am more a child of my time than I
like to think I am.

But it is interesting to be caught up in the phenomenon. Biographies that aim to 'tell it all' are also popular.
I largely approve, though it may be that we are indulging
the exhibitionist and voyeur in us all; and of course,
strictly speaking, it is impossible to tell it *all*. So, while it
seems a good thing to cut into our collusions and projec-
tions over heroes and gurus, it does raise the question,
Are there any secrets left? Is nothing private now? What
are the boundaries between public and private when institutional confidentiality is no more, in churches as well as
in hospitals?

Any one of us may wish to keep secrets, either because we
have broken the law and not yet been found out, whether
we feel guilty about it or would want to appeal to a higher
justice, or we bear a hidden stigma that would bring us
shame if the neighbours knew, or we wish to protect the privacies of an intimate relationship. I have no desire in this
book, nor do I feel any obligation, to tell it all. And there
may be some confidences that we wish to respect even when
the person who shared them has died. In a famous interview

that Carl Jung gave to John Freeman in the television series *Face to Face* not long before he died, he courteously but firmly refused to divulge what Freud had said to him about a dream, even though Freud had been dead for twenty years, and the two of them had been in Freud's later years hardly the best of friends. I find myself wanting to respect that refusal.

❖

As I grew up I remember becoming more at ease in the public than in the domestic arena. My parents did well in giving me security and protection, nourishment and encouragement, but something inside me very early on knew that they were largely irrelevant to my discovering my own life path. In retrospect I think they were more nomadic and nonconformist than circumstances let them be, and they certainly moved home many times in their last thirty years. That may have affirmed what was becoming clear to me, that I was not putting down roots in the place of my birth, that I was not a local and neighbourhood person, that home was likely to be little more than a base, at best a refreshing oasis. Though I like that base to feel homely and pleasant, I have never been engaged for long with gardens and interior decorating. The distant horns are always sounding.

I knew when I was six or seven that the world out there could be very exciting, however shy and fearful I usually was at that age, not being adept at ball games or relaxed enough for rough and tumble. It was prize day at my infants' school, and I went up on the stage, to receive what and for what I cannot now remember from a retired local dignitary, a colonel with a moustache I think. My arm was in a sling, following a bite from my best friend's dog, and when asked, "What happened to you, young man?" I whispered, "A dog bit me." The head teacher leant over to tell me to speak up because the colonel was hard of hearing. So I shouted, "A dog bit me," at which said gentleman reeled backwards and all the Mums and Dads laughed. I left the stage with a secret smile on my face, chuffed to learn that I could affect an audience. I tucked that piece of information away for later use. Within the public world, however wary I might have to be, I would find a place more stimulating and reliable than home.

I think that one of the panics of my illness was the fear that the public world would be closed to me, that I would have to retreat into complete privacy before I was ready. I have not yet thoroughly come to terms with the ambivalences of 'home'. I knew I wanted to make a public comeback, not least through writing again, and I spent some time searching for some notes of addresses on hospitality which I had given a few months before falling ill. I thought I had lost them for good, and I knew I did not have the energy or concentration needed to think through the theme afresh. It was a great relief to me when my secretary discovered them, and, once found, they provided me with the stimulus I needed to put them into shape and bring out the book *Love Rekindled* a few months later.

I was already rejoicing with George Herbert, again in his poem 'The Flower':

> And now in age I bud again,
> After so many deaths I live and write;
> I once more smell the dew and rain,
> And relish versing ...

You helped to launch *Love Rekindled* in London, and you read that poem as a 'welcome back' to me, and capped it, to the chuckling sympathy of the audience, with "Lulu's back in Town." I remembered my secret smile ...

With this ambivalence I have about public and private and the boundaries between the two, it is perhaps not surprising that I have sought to write about two issues which again are both public and private, with boundaries that have been changing rapidly this century, for bane *and* blessing; religion and sexuality. It has been hard to know how much about my own belief, and how much about my relationships, it is prudent to protect with high walls of privacy. I suspect I have sometimes been too quick to speak of both. Suffice to say here that the wind in the sails is urging me to work afresh at these things (and perhaps do some re-positioning!)

Of recent years my home has had a limited public dimension, with hospitality offered for prayer and short retreats. So the boundaries of public and private have had to be worked out in relation to quite specific rooms. At one level it has meant that the work I have done has been more private than a vicar's in and from a vicarage, at another level more public because the results of a laboratory experiment in prayer and hospitality have been written up and let loose in the world as books. Perhaps the time has emerged to be more private *and* more public, but in new spaces, with the boundaries more clearly defined. I think my friends and support group are determined not to let me become drained by too much giving, nor too isolated by public role, indeed to encourage me to be more at home at home as well as in the wider world.

As to sexuality, I am only too aware of ambivalent boundaries, of complex issues, and of a generation confused and uncertain. It is a truism to say that we are more relaxed and open than our forebears in talking about these things, though I suspect conversation flows more easily in cities than in market towns and on small islands. With less guilt and shame, we are exploring an area of sexual relating that is between the compulsive and compelling at one end (which nearly everyone would want to guard against) and the monogamously committed (and even for procreation only) at the other. We are refusing the categories of our ancestors, and of some of our contemporaries, that any sexual relationships not within marriage are automatically to be labelled as 'promiscuity 'or 'fornication'. With sex no longer necessarily connected with conception, and despite the shoals of sexually transmitted disease, with prudence and responsibility we are navigating seas where rough water may be damaging but can be exhilarating.

Of course there are dangers. Those keen to extol the merits of experiment collude with one another in sharing selective stories of how marvellous is the new freedom, while hiding any evidence of pain and damage. Those keen to preserve traditional ways hide evidence of domestic violence and turn protection of the young into an excuse for that ignorance which is still more widespread than we believe. There are few safe semi-public but off-the-record places where we can all be open enough with one another to discover what are genuine advances and what are genuine cautions.

For those who have no central other person in their lives, there is the danger of energy spread thinly, exhaustingly wide. May Sarton recognized this. Despite close friends who made her birthday memorable, she had to live through a sense of deprivation after they had gone, and she knew that "a life extended in a thousand directions risks dispersion and madness." She is writing of creative energy expended in her work of poetry and meeting people, but our sexual energy is always intimately bound up with it.

Warnings granted, including the pains of betrayal of relationships of sexual faithfulness, there is nevertheless witness to memorable moments of encounter, where pleasure and bodily affirmation have been shared, and sometimes healing and a spur to creativity, even if the encounter is never repeated. Serendipity sex? I think Dennis Potter hinted at the quality of such moments in an unpublished radio talk in 1977 and quoted by Michael Mayne in his book on his experiences of chronic fatigue syndrome, *A Year Lost and Found*:

> Whenever we play games, or act, or sing, or dance, or make love, we are 'outside' normal time. We are in the cauldron of the actual minute, and we have suspended or evaded the claims of any other moment except this one.

Such moments are not scratching the itch of lust and treating the other as disposable Kleenex. They are intensely personal moments, out of which each person emerges enlarged. They may not be the encounters of 'homo domesticus' or 'homo romanticus', but cannot be dismissed disparagingly as 'homo sporadicus'. Perhaps they are the acts of 'homo serendipitus'. (With apologies to those who bewail a fall in standards in the use of Latin and Greek as much as I would of those in the use of English!)

Something more is at work, that something which is at the core of the argument that all sex should be 'procreative'. It is hinted at in another, this time anonymous, quotation in May Sarton's journal: "What we are not drives us to consummation." It is the sense that our sexuality is most profoundly concerned with what is not yet, with an unknown future that is greater than ourselves or anything we could conceive. (Interesting word that wrote itself!)

An acquaintance of mine used the word 'metasexual' to contain some of these thoughts. We are beginning to appreciate something new as our consciousness is raised. I think he meant it to be something like 'sublimation', a creative use of sexual energy that is not directly genital but recognizes its sexual nature. Whether that implies lifelong abstention from sexual intercourse is not clear. Certainly there can be a conscious use of sexual desire, perhaps a distillation, in the solo creativity of wordcraft, the love-making of patient attention to and passionate engagement with words, parallel to soil and plants for gardeners, clay for potters, ingredients for cooks. These are all ways, as Pierre Teilhard de Chardin put it over sixty years ago, of using the fire in the basement to warm the whole house (rather than dousing it at the first opportunity, in case it gets out of hand and burns the whole house down.)

Now some would claim that this use of sexual energy is further charged by its expression genitally, not least because sexual intercourse can release creative energy *and* because it never delivers all that it promises. There is always this sense of 'something more' in the future. The disappointment, the sadness, the longing are inevitable, but that is no reason to refuse what *can* be given.

There is more to sex than child bearing, than bonding, than nurturing relationships and healing emotional wounds. Is it the sexual journey of the pilgrim soul, dimly aware that there is a yet-to-be *glorious* dimension to our human flesh? Can we work ourselves free of our desires to possess and to dominate, to cling and to submit, with or without a life partner, becoming 'metasexuals' who can ride the waves of genital encounter without *necessarily* betraying and wounding, not needing to be totally abstinent in obedience to a law which has in the past genuinely sought to protect the boundaries of love? Maybe a different kind of protection is needed, the nomadic pilgrim relating to oasiskeeper to give frame and continuity, both in their different ways content and creative with each other *and* with large draughts of solitude. The boundaries *are* shifting, the questions are alive. The answers are as yet unclear. I continue to press the question gently to myself, including it in all the disturbances about boundaries that my illness has brought more obviously into my own light of day.

I SHALL BE WHO I SHALL BE   That is another way of putting it, another version of that everything-and-nothing revelation of God usually translated as 'I Am Who I Am'. Martin Buber once elaborated it further, giving it associations of action and encounter as well as the future reference; 'I Shall Be There For You As I There For You Shall Be'. I can find room to breathe in such an enigmatic, puzzling

God, now hidden, now ablaze in a bush, now striding on ahead in cloud and pillar of fire. I have been through so much disturbance that I am more comfortable with a God of discomfort than I used to be. And in the human encounters through my illness I glimpsed a snapshot, I tasted the first fruits, of the Commonwealth of God that has yet to be fully brought into existence. I have not exactly been given the Freedom of the City of God, but I do qualify for entry, my passport stamped with the two diplomas of stigma. Nobodies can range everywhere in that city, discovering that there is no part of it where they are not at home.

I have already said that I have felt that more than we know is going on in what is going on. It may have simply been coincidence – or it may have been part of a patterning we rarely see – it may even have been that I *knew* without being aware of it, that I could 'break down' at that particular moment because enough help would come my way that summer – but it felt strange to realize that *at the right time* there was a friend of wise perception and medical experience, another at ease in psychiatric wards, and a third on sabbatical for whom I provided an unexpected case study of professional carers under stress. What is *really* going on is beyond us (beyond our ken, beyond our imagination, beyond our present, beyond the realities known by our senses) and is bigger than all of us. The whole that is God is greater than the sum of the parts that are you and me and everybody else.

All this now seems to me to almost 'matter of fact'. I certainly do not want to claim an experience of mystical intoxication nor to exaggerate the awfulness of the darkness: others have had far worse times than I did. Nevertheless, such experiences are uniquely awful for the one who undergoes them, and the gifts at their heart, whether unwrappable in this life or not, are unique too. But I do hear a faint murmuring to echo this somewhat 'gushing' passage written by Teilhard de Chardin:

> I stepped down into the most hidden depths of
> my being, lamp in hand and ears alert, to dis-
> cover whether in the deepest recesses of the
> blackness within me I might not see the glint of
> the waters of the current that flows on, whether
> I might not hear the murmur of the mysterious
> waters that rise from the uttermost depths, and
> will burst forth no one knows where. With ter-
> ror and intoxicating emotion, I realized that my
> poor trifling existence was one with the immen-
> sity of all that is and all that is in the process of
> becoming.

O.K. ... Fine ... Pass the marmalade ...

Immediately I want to turn to the humdrum and the everyday, and to that subtle temptation to claim (on our own or
on others' behalf) that we are 'special' in God's eyes,
favoured and privileged at the expense of others. No, and a
thousand times No.

At the same time as I was in the doldrums, slowly stretching back into life, a seventeen year old young woman known
to a friend of mine in Melbourne was diagnosed with depression, and three weeks later she took her own life. I
could *never* say (nor should anyone even breathe it on my
behalf) that my life was spared because it is more valuable
than hers, or that God chose to pull me through and did
nothing for her. That would be a blasphemy and make God
out to be a capricious tyrant. I want nothing to do with such
a notion.

Again, during the time of my illness, two people I know
in this country, both with the same name, one of whom I
have been friendly with for years, the other of more recent
acquaintance, both have been enduring the aftermath of severe strokes in early middle age. Again, moral or spiritual
comparisons are odious.

It remains a mystery why two people with identical symptoms, say with specific cancers and similar prognoses, should live, one for weeks, the other for years. We never *can* know the details of the complex mix of factors that have resulted in who I am now and who you are now, and how the future will unfold for each of us. With a slightly different mix of ingredients, slightly different proportions, a meal can give agonising bellyache or contented belly rumbles. I do not know what tips the balance one way, and what tips it another. Nobody does. Nobody ever can.

With all the possible variants (think of what a range of music a few notes can produce), with the unchangeable givens and the freedom of choices, we shall *never* be able to make exact calculations and predictions. We human beings remain mysterious, and I for one am glad that it is so. I want there to be an open future, even if it means not knowing of the darknesses we are one day going to enter. Perish everything in theology or in medicine that is glib and simplistically confident.

I think there is room in this approach for an unpredictable Spirit, for a Wind that blows where it wills. I do get angry at what to me is disproportionate pain and unnecessary suffering, above all in the lives of young children, and particularly where genetic malfunction is concerned, but none of us has a complete picture. I cry out in complaint that the world is as it is, and I am sometimes comforted by believing in a pain-bearing, long-suffering, love-making God. But I believe only by the narrowest of squeaks, and mainly because any other interpretation of life seems even more perplexing and awful. Grudgingly too, I make a nod before the notion of a God who is participating in the groaning of creation and working towards a wonder and a glory in which all our pains will be pinpricks. But I still ask, Is it worth the cost? I recognize there is a graciousness in the One who is greater than I not imposing a premature dénouement with a firework spectacle of omnipotence, but withdrawing, enabling our maturing, preserving and encouraging our personal response and responsibility, and bearing the unresolved for as long as it takes. I can recognize too that I might well not have understood even this much without the Jesus who embraced the outcast and died an outcast's death, whose touch and speech kindled a spark of eternal life in those who welcomed him, who gave us a decisive clue that evil, pain, and death were not the last word with God. It is just about enough to make living with unanswerable questions bearable, and, on good days, hopeful. In time, faith may touch even the worst of days ...

Ah, I have been distracted again from the humdrum and everyday, the ingredients in my particular experience that did make a difference. If there was a divine protection at work, if sufficient connections were in place, not completely torn asunder, then it was through *people* that it happened. All that I said under the heading of *Web trembling* is relevant here, but there are a few underlinings to be made. If God was up to anything at all, it was through creating the conditions in a universe that could, with no guarantees that they would, lead over the millennia to there being sufficient resources, at the right time and in the right places, available for me, enough, barely enough it is true and yet enough, to keep me from total dislocation and death.

Now this has nothing to do with the status in God's eyes of belief or unbelief. If all humanity are inextricably bound up together, then it does not ultimately *matter* how and when I die, or whether or not friend or carer is of a particular shade of belief or none. What does matter and does lessen the pain and does help healing and the knitting together of flesh and relationships torn apart, is that we move towards one another in compassion and not against one another in confrontation. And if there is a God, the rest is up to the Divine Weaver herself.

Peter de Vries wrote a novel about the death of a child, *The Blood of the Lamb*. Here is the narrator reflecting:

"Some poems are long, some are short. She was a short one," Miss Halsey said. Again the throb of compassion rather than the breath of consolation; the recognition of how long, how long is the mourner's bench on which we sit, arms linked in undeluded friendship, all of us brief links ourselves in the eternal pity.

If you have read thus far, you will be aware that I feel particular links of fellow feeling with certain writers, and that one of those is May Sarton. In her occasional journals, she was a deft, accurate, honest observer of herself, her friends, and her garden. She had known human love in its lesbian form, and all the emotional heights and depths of such a primary relationship. She also came to value friendship very highly. She might have agreed with Aelred of Rievaulx that God is Friendship. In one of her last journals, *Endgame*, she wrote a poem at Christmas 1990 with the title *Friendship and Illness*. I want to quote it here with gratitude to my own friends who did answer the question in the last stanza of the poem. Through them even awkward old God may have answered.

> Through the silences
> The long empty days
> You have sat beside me
> Watching the finches feed,
> The tremor in the leaves.
> You have not left my mind.
>
> Friendship supplied the root –
> It was planted years ago –
> To bring me flowers and seed
> Through the long drought.
> Far-flung as you are
> You have seemed to sit beside me.
> You have not left my mind.

Will you come in the new year?
To share the wind in the leaves
And the finches lacing the air
To savour the silence with me?
It's been a long time.

Yes to that: to human flesh and blood an embodied presence
is always that bit more than the disembodied voice, however
much the telephonic second best is appreciated too. A letter
came to me as the zephyrs began to stir, with these words:
"Good simply doesn't exist until it is embodied, that is, until
someone *does* it and *is* it. No amount of saying 'Jesus loves
you' makes someone feel loved ... but saying 'I love you'
commits the sayer."

When you have built up enough strength after an illness,
that love can take a necessary astringent form for our deeper healing. The judgment – better, the discernment – of
God needs embodying too, and it is still an aspect of love.

Again, about that time of emerging, I was struck by this
from a manuscript sent to me with the title *Light and Silence:
Painting, Poetry, and the Sacred:*

> We need someone to look at us intently to dis-
> cern the faith in us (Acts 14.9) – *looking intently
> and seeing beyond*, the man or woman of God
> who looks into our soul but who sees with God's
> love and draws out what is in us of God.
> Looking intently and seeing beyond is some-
> thing I do when I paint.

(Such cleansing points me back to what I wrote earlier in
this chapter under the heading *Reality*. It is discovering and
being discovered by what is *real* that is vital.)

I find it interesting that I have been drawn to one poet of
the spiritual life this past year and not to another whom I
might have expected to have been nudged by. I have been

helped by – and I have quoted from – T. S. Eliot's *Four Quartets* on a number of occasions in the past, but from George Herbert recently. I wonder. Is Eliot too elegant, the quartets too rounded, too complete with enlightenment, the truth arrived at by silence and by knowledge rather than the truth arrived at by turmoil and by pain, the still pool of the present moment rather than the ruffled waves of time and story, the word (however recognized to be inadequate) in place rather than the messiness of a love that touches the untouchable?

That may be unfair, but my journey's companion May Sarton startled me by writing this, with which I conclude this incomplete section about the elusive divine. She refers to a friend who

> ... buries herself in the *Four Quartets* but is afraid of the depression they bring on, and she assented when I suggested that Eliot's is a negative view because (I dare to think) he was not a believer. Never is the joy of religion expressed, never is there transcendence. I remember seeing *Murder in the Cathedral* when it was first produced in London in a tiny theatre. I left in a kind of black rage, because I had been put through a wringer but there had been no catharsis. The choruses especially left nothing but sand in my mouth. But that is why Eliot had such an influence in the twenties when people did not want to hear good news, at least not good religious news. The 'Zeitgeist' was violently against such a view as George Herbert's, but now we go back to him who never denied the desert in himself but pierces us still with the humanness of his faith and his intimate relationship with his God, often complaining but never arid for long. He was a believer, and that is the huge difference.

❖

NOT KNOWING YET HOPING   A friend asked, "Do you think you have been through a dark night of the soul?" I drew back from the thought. That sort of thing is for the spiritual élite, and in any case I have found myself rather steering clear of John of the Cross – all that Spanish intensity and heat of the sun. I had also been startled, again in that densely packed exploding month before I became ill, by somebody coming up to me after a workshop in Glasgow and saying, "It's not often you get to meet a mystic."

Turn the megaphone off, *please*. Let me tone that down, and take to myself a truth and a possibility. It was certainly a 'dark night'. And we may well be entering an age of 'ordinary mystics'. Just as religious communities have guarded the human values of solitude, silence, and simplicity through the promises of chastity, obedience, and poverty, and for centuries of fear and guardedness have kept the 'pilgrim souls' alive and moving, but may now be releasing their truth into the wider community because it is vital for human survival and flourishing that more of us should sit lightly to family, information, and possessions, yet include our sexuality in a more embodied way, so it may be that approaches to contemplation and creativity once confined to those who took it on for life are now becoming part of the spiritual equipment of ordinary folk. And there *is* something of the 'mystic' in every artist, whether working with wood or paint, words or sounds. I also have to admit that a line of John of the Cross did come my way at a useful time in my darkness – that we have to travel an unknown path to arrive at what we do not yet know. Come to think of it, Eliot used that thought: I mustn't be too hard on him!

Our trouble is that we inherit and accumulate so much mental and emotional clutter (as well as material possessions) and in the practical tasks of keeping going we so easily push away what we feel we have no time for (we do what is urgent not what is important), and the attic and cellars fill up with boxes of the neglected. Yes, we need to be emptied, we need a serious if not stark simplicity, a certain stillness, a measure of silence, a degree of solitude: the pruning process is a kind of darkening, but a way to discovering a more intense light.

Another question I was asked was this: Could I see the light at the end of the tunnel? (I resisted the morose response that the light might be the headlamp of an approaching train.) But again the question did not quite fit. I was in the dark certainly, but it was only after long months that I could say that I was no longer *stuck* in the dark. I might be still much of the time, resting, recovering, but I was no longer paralyzed and rigid. I had started to *move*, slowly and gradually beginning to examine the clutter. At first, the moves were tentative. I stumbled, groping my way by sound and touch, unsteady, unsure. It could be that I have learned to visit the dark and be more at ease there. I have been learning to see in a new way. A Russian holy man was convinced he was called to "keep his soul in hell and not despair". Again, that sounds too extra-ordinary for me, but dwelling in the dark when needed, to cradle my inner infant to sleep, to wait for a new illumination, to discover hidden treasure, to make it one of the stopping-places of the nomad-pilgrim, and still to keep faith, and to find glowing there the embers of hope ...

The task of writing this book has been part of that clearing process. Three months or so ago, in early spring, it began to press upon me. I knew then that the time was ripe. When the final proofs have gone to the printer, I shall breathe a huge sigh of relief. I will have cleared some very important space, some of which I hope I can keep empty, so that I can both endure and enjoy a new 'not knowing' (and of course I hope the book sells *very* well, and brings some money in for a modicum of fun!) The challenge is to become like the bird watcher in a hide: still, silent, relaxed, yet aware and alert for the minutest movements and the tiniest sounds. Then the new and unexpected will trust us enough to reveal themselves and draw near.

❖

As in the previous sections, here are some companions from the wider world who comfort and encourage me. That redoubtable contemplative pray-er of the Sisters of the Love of God, Mary Clare, once wrote:

> The contemplative dimension is the fruit of our willingness to meet the discipline of learning to wait in silence and stillness, as well as the boredom and loneliness and sometimes the apparent emptiness which confronts us in the waiting.

The American monk Thomas Merton wrote to the Russian novelist Boris Pasternak a letter which I find moving, given the political circumstances of the time and the antagonistic relationship between their two countries. As I read it with my own recent experience in mind, it is another nudge: Choose silence or it will be forced upon you.

> May you find again within yourself the deep life giving silence which is genuine truth and the source of truth: for it is a fountain of life and a window into the abyss of eternity and God. It is the wonderful silence of the winter night in which Yurii sat up in the sleeping house and wrote his poems while the wolves howled outside: but it is an inviolable house of peace, a fortress in the depths of our being, the virginity of our soul where, like the blessed Mary, we give our brave and humble answer to life, the 'Yes' which brings Christ into the world.

❖

A playwright is next, Dennis Potter again, from his radio talk. There is less 'religion' here, which appeals to me:

> I feel ... that the world is being made right in front of us, and we stand always at the edge of

this creation, and in living out our lives give back piece by piece what has been given us to use and work and wrestle with. We shape our own lives and find our own humanity in the long passage from premonitions of innocence through the darkness of mortal distress, carelessness, and apparent absurdity into the light we know is there if we have the patience and the courage to be still, to concentrate – to be alert ...

All is well. Not by facile optimism, not in blinkered evasions, but in the richest and most active dimension of our humanity. It is the illumination we must and will ever seek on the other side of the dark.

The image changes, to that of the unimaginable treasure beyond all the confusion, darkness, and disintegration. Hope is alive again, of an indestructible love and life that can never be erased or destroyed, pure diamond waiting for the light to burst into colour and flame.

For now, it is also a matter of faith, of living with the questions, with doubts, vulnerable to the accusations of the napalmed child. But the ember does glow in the darkness.

Change the image again: undiscovered creatures swim in the dark depths of the ocean, seen only by those who can bear to take the deepest soundings with equipment that has never been tested at such pressure ... Without hope no one would venture, or, as Albert Camus said, "In the midst of winter I discovered that there was in me an invincible summer." The 'not knowing' and the hope flower into a new fulfilment.

And last, Oliver Sacks stretches my imagination with yet fresher hope of what *can* happen, though we hardly believe it, and it leaves us with a considerable 'not yet' of understanding, another dimension of 'not knowing'. Perhaps its name is 'wonder'.

> One must allow the possibility of an almost limitless repertoire of functional reorganizations and accommodations of all types, from cellular, chemical, and hormonal levels to the organization of the self – the 'will to get well'. One sees again and again ... (in) all the diseases, remarkable, unexpected, and 'inexplicable' resolutions, at times when it seems that everything is lost. One must allow – with surprise and delight – that such things happen – *Why* they should happen, and *what* indeed is happening, are questions which it is not yet in our power to answer; for health goes deeper than any disease.

The gifts from the darkness – from who knows how long a silent expectant waiting, on our own or others' behalf; and we never know where next the bush will burst into flame, the water gush from the rock, the seeds on the desert floor bloom again.

❖

TIME AND PACE   I experience time differently now. So far I've thought of three changes.

The first is that it is always five to midnight. Having brushed death, I know the wings are never far away. Life is more fragile and precarious than ever. Anything I do is provisional – as are arrangements, more in pencil in the diary now than in ink.

I felt it more acutely, this entering the last border country, if only, for the time being, for a brief visit, because my mother had now died as well as my father.

There is no longer a generation in front of me, no buffer any more.

At the same time, and this is the second change, the surge of recovered energy has made me cherish the prospect of a good number of years to come, and therefore to acknowledge and act on the gift. Keep healthy as far as in you lies, so that you avoid coronaries, cancers and strokes, and one day in your late eighties, slip away on a summer evening while watching the sunset, a half-eaten smoked salmon hors d'oeuvre at my side. Well, I can but dream!

There are other questions to live with too – choosing which invitations to say Yes to; pacing them, travelling more leisurely, resting afterwards; limiting but absorbing what comes my way; relishing, cherishing, savouring; ripening rather than merely getting older; taking note of how much stamina and resilience I have; dealing with whatever from the past still damages the present, but not constantly and anxiously delving the darkness – enjoying the sun as well, letting the warmth melt fear, letting the light transfigure the dark in its own time; being quiet and still in turning to inner and outer light; letting the Why question be, while treasuring and acting upon whatever insights I have discovered and been given; easing off control and understanding and systems – love the fragments, love yourself in your own fragments; treat yourself kindly – even in your less appealing habits and moods; letting the resolutions and new patterns emerge as the waters of the stream quieten down from the spate of floods; doing less, but with more singularity; not inflicting too many words on the world, so creating in others another set of expectations for me to dance to; playing with Jimmy in the sand.

The third aspect of my changed sense of time is that there is always enough for today, and enough resource for what is

needed for today. (I write as one of the fortunate ones who
has not fallen into destitution, however much my worst
state mirrored it and made me anxious that I would be
homeless within two years.)

It is the gift, the gem, of the present moment. On the
Sustrans bicycle ride last summer, I was often asked, "How
far are you going?" I usually replied, "The next mile," and
after a pause for perplexed amazement, went on, "And if I
enjoy that, then the next one. If, barring foul weather,
snarled chain, and raw groin, I greet the Atlantic Ocean at
Land's End in the middle of August, I shall allow myself a
moment or two of exultation and sense of achievement. But
I shan't feel a miserable wimp and failure if a railway station
en route beckons me with welcoming arms." (Actually, that
little speech is a considerable exaggeration: I simply enjoyed
writing it as I chuckle and remember. But the point remains; how hard – but what a pleasure – to live fully in the
moment.)

A story is told of a nun who borrowed a bicycle from one
of her sisters because she was late for Mass at the local
church. In her haste she left it unlocked outside against the
railings near the porch. As she left after the service she was
chatting away and fell easily into her usual walk home, not
remembering the bicycle until the following morning. She
ran to the church – and the bicycle was still there. Thanks
be to God! She went into the church to light a candle of
gratitude, and when she came out, the bike had gone …

Dennis Potter

> came to understand that God … is not an unc-
> tuous palliative, or a super-pill, or a sugary
> abstraction, but … someone present in the quick
> of being, one's own being, and in the present
> tense itself, in existence as it exists, in the fibre
> and pulse of the world, and in the minute-by-
> minute drama of an ever-continuing, ever-
> poised, ever-accessible creation.

I have never liked being asked, "Are you happy?" I want to answer in someone else's words again, but I've forgotten whose, "No, but I'm not unhappy about it." Now I have come to recognize that happiness is not a state but a moment. There will be in *today* a moment to be recognized as a moment of happiness, to be caught on the wing, warmed by my hands, and let go of – with a kiss – to the skies.

STRANDS ... CAIRNBUILDING   It is impossible to finish this book, but I am about to stop.

There is no neat way of rounding off these descriptions and reflections. The controller cannot win. I sometimes feel as if I have been holding a jelly, passing it from hand to hand because the maker of moulds is on holiday. At best I may have given *some* shape to *some* of what has been happening – and some to the questions I have been contemplating, an exploration that has opened up such mysterious territory that I find myself feeling further away than ever from any answers. I have more to learn from that terrain before I can claim to have 'lived into' such partial answers as may be waiting to be given.

Your image for me was that of a transformation from frightened rabbit (blinded by too much terror – and rage – and by too much light) to bouncing hare. I need not scuttle away into the dark warren, or be dragged back concussed by the ambulance service of the meadows, and I need to take care not to leap and stride too quickly, too often, or too much driven by compulsion.

Writing this book has been part of the task of reorientation, of finding new signposts, of building new cairns. My hope is that it will help others as well as myself who have been

startled and bewildered, help us in the never-ending quest
to bring order out of formlessness, harmony out of chaos.
This is bound to be difficult for us all in an age where there
are few well-trodden paths for us to follow, when the cairns
have to be built, not merely followed.

To be *alive* in these present times is to become aware that
we can no longer fully identify ourselves by our particular
religion or nation, hard as it is to resist the temptation to
fall back into such separatisms, to survive only at the expense of being over against others and feeling superior to
them. I think I have emerged from this illness less completely Christian and less completely English. I find myself,
both intuitively and practically, a citizen of a global society,
even if Jim Cotter plc is not the most obvious multi-nation-
al! The nomad-pilgrim lives *towards* new patterns of faith
and community, towards a future not yet born, a seed scat-
terer who may never know what will take root and grow. I
am still moved by singing William Blake's 'Jerusalem' as I
cross the border south from Scotland, but I am glad of the
increasing freedom of movement across old boundaries, and
I am even more moved by another anthem/hymn from Paul
Winter's *Missa Gaia*, which has the travellers of the future
looking on that blue and white sphere from space and
knowing that it is their home.

It is costly living in a change time where the old boundaries are dissolving and the unresolved hurts of the past are
clamouring for healing. The Earth and the children of
Earth cry out in pain. When we live in an age which does
not have the safety nor the wisdom to manage with calm,
nor patiently put right, what has gone wrong, there is too
much 'in the air', there are too many invisible arrows, there
are too many hidden landmines. Minor hates and grudges
accumulate, sometimes over centuries, for example each
citizen of Europe adding to the Church's shame in our
attitude to the Jews, and suddenly – amidst perplexity –

those 'powers' of oppression coalesce into systematic genocide.

That is one of the issues that I *know* I have to (am 'called' to) take to heart. Born at the time of the construction of Auschwitz, I cannot extract myself from its consequences nor avoid trying to keep alive the memories until such times as the roots of our hatred have withered, and so no longer have power to harm.

'Prayer' in such circumstances may be our awareness and identification with such pain, with the atmosphere it has left behind, with the connection with our own unredeemed desires to scapegoat others. We may subsequently *act* as well, but we may well be stirring and moving 'waves' of healing simply by being and standing, 'contemplating', our apparent passivity hard to endure for those of us fond of using imagination and creative words. To bear the disturbance and not to pass it on is to begin to transform it. The energy at its heart is not necessarily bad, but it does need to be released from its *vicious* circles, and, re-directed, become creative again. (That may be something of what the old stories of 'Lucifer', 'Light-Bearer', were getting at.)

I am *now* aware that I have entered such territory too much in my own ego strength, too unprotected, the sensitivity of a missing layer of skin both making me more aware and also more vulnerable. It is perilous work to try to hold the evil and the good together, hard to be steady and unafraid in the darkness, knowing your capacity for destruction of others and of yourself. When such work has not been clear of my own personal agendas, my own entanglements with the unresolved past, the dangers have increased. I may too easily walk into another's space, unaware of the buffetings that will come at me, blithely entering because I hope that unmet needs of my own will be recognized and fed.

So my own protected times and spaces become vital, for a regular, frequent, and steady turning towards the Sun, towards the Accepting and Sustaining One, the ultimate Mystery, the Giver of Life, Bearer of Pain, Maker of Love.

Otherwise, the visits to the cellar will be damaging and the slowly growing mushrooms and bulbs will be trampled. The doors and windows of the house of my being need draught excluders and double glazing to keep the sound and fury at bay during the worst of times. It is *so stupid* to keep them open *all* day and *all* night and in *every* season of the year.

So it feels all right again to do a little gentle rubbish clearing, from a filing cabinet with dead weight from the past in it, to distilling, as slowly as a maturing single malt, what my companions of book and body are contributing to my life, tasting, waiting, then either spitting (casting away, re-cycling, giving away, selling) or swallowing and absorbing: even then, there is always some more eliminating to be done.

Through this process, this absorbing in my guts, this taking to my heart, there may be something to give to the new century whose first light is already in the eastern sky. It is but a few days short of the summer solstice as I write this, looking north over the sea *from* Skye. When there are no clouds there is no darkness at all above the northern rim of the horizon. Perhaps with my new sense of time, it is not only five *to* midnight but five *past* midnight. Already the *first* light is glowing orange, and work is being done long before most people are up and about. At this latitude at this time of year, at this time in the twenty-four hours, a bird is singing. There is no need for a watchman to keep faith in the darkness; there is a gentle stirring of what is new, a breeze in the air, a silken and courteous roll of a hesitant wave lapping the pebbles on the shore.

My companions on this so awful yet hopeful journey – face to face when you were able, ear to ear by telephone, through the pages of what you have written, encouragers known and unknown, alive now or of a previous generation, soft tremblers of the web of prayer across the physical separations of distance and of death – you have all been my *saving grace*. As I have been writing these past days, the weather has closed in once or twice, and with the sea restless and grey and no land between me and the Arctic cold, I have felt the shudders of fears and fantasies. But it has cleared again, and even the waters of the Hebrides have been calm. From time to time you my companions have appeared – dinghies and coastal cargo vessels, speedboats and elegantly refurbished training ships (take your pick!). The colours have slanted, the dancing light has given delight, and an amazing variety of rocks on the beach have been the easy quarry for an unusual cairn or two.

But it is *your* cairns that have helped me most, and much of this book has been a description of them. And that is how I want to end (or stop), with yours and not with mine. Your names first, and then your cairns: Thomas Merton, active contemplative of America, David Wood of the Community of the Three Hours in Cumbria, Loren Eiseley, evocative naturalist of America and Peter Heidtmann who wrote of him, the writer of an epitaph on a grave at Capel-y-ffin, and Geoffrey Dearmer, shy and little known poet of the First World War who died as my own life-restoring breezes began to blow again:

> And in all this we have to retain a balance and a good sense which seems to require a miracle, and yet they are the fruit of ordinary grace ...

> We are giving birth out of the top of our heads and so giving birth to no new thing, only the repeated mutations of our tired minds. Not from the belly of the Spirit ...

Eiseley could never forget the void out of which
the world emerged, nor that the earth itself contains ... the dark heart of nothingness, from
which springs all that lives ...

... [the individual] seems almost a lens, a gathering point through which, in some psychic and
unexplainable manner, is projected a portion of
the diversified and terrific forms of nature that
otherwise stream helplessly away without significance to humanity.
    Individuals who can serve this lenslike func-
tion are few in number.

Not only must they be gifted in the use of words
in order to communicate with the rest of us;
they must also [in Eiseley's view] feel the call of
the wilderness ...

Our very addiction to the day and our compulsion, manifest throughout the ages, to invent
and use illuminating devices, to contest with
midnight, to cast off sleep as we would death,
suggest that we know more of the shadows than
we are willing to recognize. We have come
from the dark wood of the past, and our bodies
carry the scars and unhealed wounds of that
transition. Our minds are haunted by night
terrors that arise from the subterranean domain
of racial and private memories ...

... in the essays verbal magic is his [Eiseley's]
ultimate resource ... he is like the primitive cast-
er of spells, hoping through words to keep at bay
the powerful forces of death and disorder that
threaten to erupt from the surrounding dark ...

❖

(Of course I warm to Loren Eiseley and hope he might recognize me as a lesser cousin – at least thrice removed – in the extended family of wordsmiths. And yet, and yet ... there is more to be said than raw courage and indomitable hard-won faith in light and life. There *are* moments of laughter, even of serene *joy*, that suggest that the midnight sun is no mere physical phenomenon of a swinging axis.)

But oh my dear
How rich and rare
And root down deep
And wild and sweet
It is to laugh ...

Amid the snarling impotence of wars
Turn where you will. Look, there a signboard shows
The lair of guns; already round the sign
White trumpeting convulvuli entwine
Their clinging arms; across the placard blows
A quiet-breathing rose.

Books by Jim Cotter

PRAYER AT NIGHT'S APPROACHING
A revised edition of Prayer at Night, *1997*

PRAYER AT NIGHT
A Book for the Darkness
Fourth edition 1988

PRAYER IN THE DAY
A Book of Mysteries
Second edition 1992

PRAYER IN THE MORNING
A Book for Day's Beginning
Second edition 1990

New unfoldings of the Psalms
published in 1989, 1991, & 1993 respectively, as
THROUGH DESERT PLACES
BY STONY PATHS
TOWARDS THE CITY

HEALING – MORE OR LESS
Reflections and Prayers at the End of an Age
Second edition, 1990

PLEASURE, PAIN, AND PASSION
Some Perspectives on Sexuality and Spirituality
Second edition, 1993

GOOD FRUITS
Same-sex Relationships and Christian Faith
Second edition 1988

YES ... MINISTER?
Patterns of Christian Service
1992

NO THANK YOU, I'M 1662
Cartoons at the Giving of the Peace
1988

LOVE REKINDLED
Practising Hospitality
1996

LOVE RE-MEMBERED
Resources for a House Eucharist
1996